MIDLAND ENGINES

No. 3 – THE CLASS 2 SUPERHEATED 4-4-0s
('483' CLASS REBUILDS)

by

DAVID HUNT, BOB ESSERY and FRED JAMES

No. 40396 hauling the Sundays only 5.43 p.m. Chester to Rhyl train past the old city walls of Chester on 19th August 1951. It was built in 1891 at Derby to O/920 as one of the '1808' Class and was originally numbered 83. In 1905 it was rebuilt with an H boiler and became 396 in 1907. It was one of the last '483' rebuilds in 1923 and was shedded at Rhyl when this photograph was taken. Since being rebuilt it had lost its bogie brakes and bypass valves, had 'pop' safety valves fitted in place of Ramsbottom ones, and acquired a few more snap-headed rivets, rain gutters and extra washout holes. It still had its original 3,250 gallon tender, No. 1958, which had built-in toolboxes, coal rails finishing at the extended front plate, short side plate extensions and separate footstep supports. In essence, though, it was the same locomotive that had been in service for 28 years and would continue for ten more.
M. ALEXANDER

WILD SWAN PUBLICATIONS

No. 508 was one of the first rebuilds carried out in 1912 and in this view typifies the appearance of the early members of the class in original condition. This picture shows how the smokebox, splasher and cab sides, with the exception of the butt strip and front edge above it, were flush riveted whereas the tops of both leading and cab splashers had snap-headed rivets. Even the front frames above the platform had only a few bolt heads protruding with the majority being flush. The capuchon chimney and dome casing were the original tall ones and the twin Ramsbottom and one lock-up safety valve bases had a long oval casing. Bogie splash guards, brakes and bypass valves were fitted and this picture shows washout doors on the shoulders of the firebox. The tender was an unmodified 3,250 gallon type with a low front, coal rails curved front and back, no side extension plates, and frame-mounted footsteps. Note, however, the unusual placement of a laterally-mounted toolbox on the right-hand side of the front plate. At first glance there don't seem to have been any tank vents but the right-hand one can just be seen above the coal. It was this that caused problems with debris getting into the tanks and blocking the filters. The lined crimson lake livery was as described in the text but note how crimson lake and black appear virtually identical to the orthochromatic film. When this is borne in mind, it becomes impossible to tell what colour the cab roof was painted. The grab handles on the locomotive platform and the pillar handrails were bare metal, whereas grab handles on the tender sides were painted; the painting or otherwise of these items varied. The unpainted fork of the reversing rod and black coupling rod fluting are evident and the Derby makers' plates can be seen on the frames below the smokebox.

AUTHOR'S COLLECTION

INTRODUCTION

Having reached the third of what we hope will be a successful series of locomotive monographs, we trust that we have eliminated the majority of the faults present in the first two and are close to 'getting it right'. That does not mean, however, that we aren't interested in criticism or comment any more – just the opposite. If you have something you want to see changed, added or deleted, please tell us about it. We can't promise to satisfy everyone individually but we can take note and react to common perceptions where possible. As an example of this process, we have been asked by several readers of previous volumes to include explanations of how some of the locomotive components to which we refer worked. Whilst we don't want to turn each book into a mechanical treatise, we will try to include some basic explanations in the text and with the notes accompanying some of the drawings.

One point we would make about the concept of these books is that they are not intended to be photographic albums of locomotives. Rather we hope they will be seen as reference works for modellers, artists and locomotive historians. Apart from cover and frontispiece photographs, the choice of a picture for reproduction has one criterion – does it illustrate what we want to highlight in the text or the drawings that form the core of the work? If a previously unpublished photograph fulfils this aim, we will use it in preference to one that has been seen before. There are, however, a finite number of acceptable quality negatives to which we have access. Thus it will often be the case that familiar views will have to be used and for this we make no apology. One thing we do hope to achieve is to enable some readers better to interpret other photographs to which they may have access.

In *Midland Engines No. 2* we listed locomotive types that we are considering as subjects for future works and made a plea for original material that may help us to achieve accuracy in writing about them. We are still interested in readers' input and are therefore reiterating that request. Types under consideration are the Class 3 goods tank engines, Compounds, 0–4–0 shunting tanks, Class 4 goods engines, '990' Class 4–4–0s, Johnson 'singles', motor train fitted engines, Class 3 Belpaire rebuilds, Class 2 goods engines, 0–6–4 passenger tank engines, H-boilered goods engines and early 0–4–4 passenger tanks. If you would like to see locomotives other than those we have referred to featured, let us know. We can't guarantee that we can find the necessary material on any particular class but we can try.

As we indicated in *Midland Engines No. 1*, we see this as part of a collectors' series and, as such, we will often refer to previous or even future issues rather than repeat information. Thus, for an explanation of the Midland's class nomenclature and engine numbering we refer readers either to the article on the '1121' Class 0–6–0 Goods tank engines in *Midland Record No. 11* or to *Midland Engines No. 2* on the Class 3 Belpaire goods locomotives.

The 157 locomotives we feature here were originally built as Johnson 'slim-boilered' 4–4–0s between 1882 and 1901.[1] In their final, rebuilt form they have been referred to as the '483' Class. This description may be a little puzzling to some readers since No. 483 was neither the first to be rebuilt with a G7S boiler, nor was it the lowest numerically. It was, in fact, the lowest numbered engine included in the first order for rebuilding, which covered Nos. 483–522 of the so-called '150' Class. However, since the nomenclature is known to have been used in Derby Works and has achieved some measure of common usage, we will refer to the engines as such. Note that we are not including the five S&DJR superheated Class 2 engines in our coverage. As usual, where we know of discrepancies between what we have written and what has been published before, we draw attention to the fact and give our source or reasoning without necessarily identifying the work with which we disagree.

The class has previously been described as having had few variations and modifications. That this is not entirely true will become apparent. Whilst we have tried to be as accurate as possible in our description of the variations and alterations they did exhibit, we cannot claim to have unearthed every detail about them. As usual, therefore, we urge modellers and artists to proceed with caution and to use photographs of their chosen engine taken at the appropriate time in order to achieve accuracy.

Once again we are indebted to Dieter Hopkin, Head of Library and Archive Collections at the National Railway Museum, for his assistance in making much hitherto unused material available to us. Similarly, without the help of Marion Berry and Phil Atkins, also of the NRM, this volume simply would not have been possible. Phil's impressively broad knowledge of locomotive matters has often pointed us in the right direction for research and made life a lot easier. The structure of the text in *Midland Engines No. 2*, which we have adopted for this volume, was suggested by David Tee and has proved to be popular, so to him we owe our thanks for that and for all the other assistance and advice he has given, which has been considerable. In particular, David has made available some of his research material on tenders and hitherto unknown, to us, letters concerning the changes to LMS liveries from 1927 to 1935. We are also grateful to Terry Essery for his professional engineman's appreciation of the class and assistance with some of the footplate details.

Bob Essery, Fred James and David Hunt

The locomotives that were rebuilt with G7 superheated boilers to become Class 483 rebuilds, or Class 2P as they were commonly known, all began life as Johnson 'slim boilered' 4–4–0s. Although they shared common design features, they were generally similar in outline, notwithstanding the fact that they had different boiler lengths, driving wheel diameters and wheelbase measurements. We illustrate No. 2201 as an example. In due course the majority of these engines were rebuilt with Class H boilers and here we illustrate an example from each series in this condition. Most but not all of these engines were to be rebuilt with G7S boilers, becoming 483 class, the subject of this book. The story is complex but fortunately it has been told in Midland Locomotives Vol. 2 – Passenger Tender Classes (Essery & Jenkinson. Wild Swan).

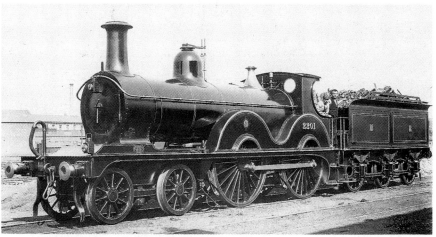

1738 Class No. 370 with H boiler – the only one to become a 483.

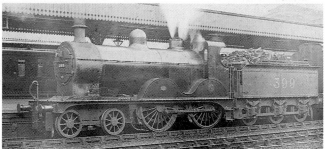

1808 Class No. 399 with H boiler in LMS period.

2183 Class No. 235 with H boiler. All 25 engines became 483s.

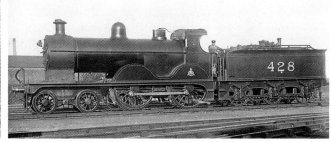

2203 Class No. 428 with H boiler. Most became 483 rebuilds.

2581 Class No. 476 with H boiler. Five became 483 rebuilds.

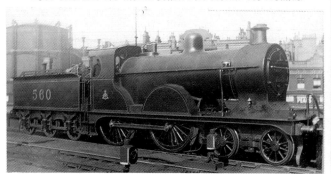

60 Class No. 560 with H boiler. All 30 engines became 483s.

150 Class No. 156 with H boiler. Series included 1667 Class renewals.

ORIGINS

AFTER S.W. Johnson took over responsibility for Midland Railway locomotive affairs in 1873, wheel arrangements on the company's new passenger tender engine stock were restricted to 2–4–0, 4–2–2 and 4–4–0 types. Up to 1881 the 2–4–0 was still being built, although some 4–4–0s had been produced in 1876 and 1877, but from 1882 onwards the leading bogie became universal. By the mid-1880s, Derby drawing office was able to design locomotives with 17 tons axle loading compared with 12 tons in the 1860s. This, together with cost and friction considerations and, most importantly, steam sanding, led to the introduction in 1887 of the first Johnson 4–2–2s. Over the following 13 years batches of 4–4–0s and 4–2–2s were built, each incorporating much the same design features and improvements as though Johnson and the Locomotive Department were unable to decide which wheel arrangement was the better. Eventually, however, the need for even more powerful, heavier locomotives with larger boilers decided against the Singles and big 4–4–0s won the day.

The turn of the century saw a major alteration in the appearance of Midland 4–4–0s. Due to the need for increased power on the heavier and sharply-timed Scotch (*sic*) expresses, the '2606' Class and, shortly afterwards, the first five Compounds were built with large boilers and Belpaire fireboxes. These were a development of the flat-topped type that had been used by William Bouch on some Stockton & Darlington Railway 0–6–0s in 1866 and their perceived advantages were increased steam space and a better arrangement of stays. They were first made in Britain by Beyer, Peacock in 1872 for a batch of 2–4–0s built for export to Spain (we made an error in *Midland Engines No. 2* by stating that these locomotives went to Belgium), and were introduced into British use on the Manchester, Sheffield & Lincolnshire Railway in 1891.

When the Midland first adopted Belpaire fireboxes, only boilers of new engines were fitted with them.

The left-hand side of an early rebuild was as shown in this photograph of an engine in photographic grey bearing the number 483. The finish enables detail to be seen quite clearly. For instance, note the covers for the piston tail rods on the top of the platform between the frames and the weighshaft bearing in the angle between the leading splasher and the frame. This picture shows the superheater damper control equipment and separate handrail on the side of the smokebox and the Silvertown mechanical lubricator on a bracket attached to the top of the left-hand frame. The tender was an unmodified 3,250 gallon one with the lateral toolbox in the usual position on the left-hand side. Details of the livery stand out clearly and the top of the upper beading on the tender sides was unlined. Note, however, that the dog ring and hinges on the smokebox and the whistle were painted, whereas they were polished metal when the real paint scheme was applied to locomotives in this condition. COLLECTION R. J. ESSERY*

The steaming capacity of most of the 'slim-boilered' 4–4–0s was increased by rebuilding them from June 1904 onwards with larger, round-topped, 175psi H boilers.[2] Within a few years, however, Derby apparently became convinced of the worth of the new firebox and Belpaire versions of existing round-topped boilers were introduced. The Belpaire equivalent of the H boiler was designated G7 and began to appear on rebuilt 4–4–0s in May 1909.

Although schemes were prepared under Deeley for Midland 4–6–0s, the company never built anything bigger than a 4–4–0 for passenger traffic.[3] Possible reasons for this 'small engine policy' have occupied vast areas of print over the years and we don't propose to go too deeply into the matter here. We do, however, feel that a short discussion of some factors would be beneficial for the reader new to Midland locomotive matters in the context of the Class 2 superheated engines.

The strength of some Midland Railway iron girder bridges was quite probably an important factor in the maximum size and power of locomotive that the company could consider economically viable. This may well have been particularly true of express

locomotives that would inflict a large 'hammer blow' on the structures. Certainly, the maximum permitted axle loading and weight per foot run on the Midland were more restrictive than on many other railways. Replacement of the bridges in question would have been a long and costly process, as indeed it was well into LMS days, and in the medium term could have denied the use of anything bigger than a Compound.[4] Economic considerations in general were beginning to have a much greater impact on the railways of Britain in the Edwardian era and locomotives represented a huge capital outlay. Therefore, providing that existing stock could be kept in good order and train weights stayed comfortably within its capabilities, building expensive, new engines could be avoided. It should be borne in mind that profitability and dividends were far more important to the business of running a railway than keeping up with the Joneses as regards the acquisition of big locomotives. Of course, the principal expresses demanded up-to-date and comfortable rolling stock run to competitive schedules in order to attract passengers and so some reasonably large and powerful engines were required – hence the

'Belpaires', Compounds and '990' Class 4–4–0s. Such trains, however, were but a small part of the company's passenger traffic and if double-heading or running trains in several portions was cheaper than strengthening lots of bridges, then so be it. Even then, relatively few of these Class 3 and 4 locomotives would suffice.

But what of the bread-and-butter passenger traffic and even the less prestigious expresses? Similar arguments could apply as regards the expense of double-heading or running more trains versus the capital outlay of bigger engines. There would, of course, come a point at which the dominant side of the equation would reverse, particularly if the majority of the motive power available was small and elderly. The cost of extra manpower, fuel and maintenance could then start to outweigh the savings. If, however, there was a compromise that could be achieved it would probably be looked on favourably by the Board.

One such compromise could have been to modernise and increase the power of some existing locomotives so that slightly greater train weights could be used without a vastly increased expenditure on genuinely new engines or manpower and maintenance. Even if such rebuilds re-used only a few components, at least some savings could have been effected (in fact, there were quite a few bits of the old engines re-used in the '483' rebuilds as will be apparent later).[5] It would also have made sense to rebuild a disparate group of engines so that they became more or less standardised and thus simplified spares holdings and maintenance with commensurate savings.

We don't claim that the above is a definitive discussion of the Midland passenger traffic characteristics, or the record of passenger locomotive building and rebuilding after 1900, but it does seem to agree with the facts as we understand them. There were other questions, such as the maintenance costs of long travel valves versus savings in coal consumption, that we consider to have affected Derby's design features but they are outside the scope of this dis-

cussion. What we do firmly believe, however, is that the men who ran the Midland Railway were not fools and they reached their decisions for sound economic and operational reasons. There were other approaches that could have been taken, such as improved infrastructure, bigger engines, heavier trains, different design features and the like, that were adopted by other railways but which were obviously not thought right for the Midland at the time. The fact that the company was at least as successful commercially as the other major railways of Britain would suggest that its policies can't have been too bad, at least in the medium term. Admittedly, the company would eventually have needed to change its ways but the distortion of railway economics brought about by the political stupidity of 1914 makes how and when imponderable questions.

Superheating provided a way of increasing the performance and economy of almost any locomotive by delaying condensation in the cylinders and thus reducing heat loss. It was first applied to a Midland locomotive in 1910 when a '990' Class 4–4–0 was fitted with a G9AS boiler.[6] The improvement was striking. Many observers have questioned the subsequent Midland policy of giving priori-

ty to superheating large numbers of small engines rather than the bigger Class 4 express locomotives. It could, however, have been seen as the means of obtaining the improvement in existing smaller 4–4–0s that we have just considered. If our suppositions are correct, its application to them would have carried a higher priority than improving the Class 4 engines. This fits in with what happened, inasmuch as the programme for rebuilding the Class 2 engines with G7S superheated boilers preceded that for superheating the more powerful passenger locomotives. In its first few years, the rate of progress was quite rapid but, because of the great 1914–1918 insanity, the rate slowed down and by the Grouping there were still many saturated steam engines in service. Although the LMS carried on with the orders placed in Midland days, the original intention of equipping all the 328–562 series with G7S boilers was never realised.[7]

Despite curtailing rebuilding of the '483s', four years after the last one was turned out from Derby the LMS began building a standard version of the design. This, we hope, will be the subject of a book in our companion series *LMS Locomotive Profiles* and so we will leave it there.

No. 517 passing a couple of young enthusiasts with camera and notebook and a pair of '1900' series bankers on the release road at Blackwell on the top of the Lickey incline in the summer of 1921. The engine was one of sixteen of its class shedded at Bristol, which were that depot's principal passenger locomotives at the time. They were also the Midland Railway's most numerous and widespread single class of 4–4–0 and, as such, played an important part in hauling the company's passenger trains.   **COLLECTION R. S. CARPENTER**

REBUILDING AND MODIFICATIONS

This picture of No. 518, taken c.1920, shows a locomotive where the superheater damper had been removed, coupled to a 3,250 gallon tender that we describe as Category 1.
AUTHORS' COLLECTION

We should use the word 'rebuilt' when describing these engines since it was the official Midland term, even though there was relatively little of the original material re-used and the main fabric was new. The first order for rebuilding, O/3942, read, 'Please put your work in hand in connection with rebuilding engines 483–522 with new frames, new cylinders and G7 boilers fitted with Schmidt's superheaters.' Apart from the savings made by using the parts that were salvaged from the old engines, there was an added benefit in referring to them as rebuilt since the royalties due to the superheater company were lower for modified locomotives than for new ones.

Of the 'slim-boilered' 4–4–0s, only the thirty Class F and G engines built in 1876 and 1877 by Kitson and Dübs retained boilers of their original basic design prior to the appearance of the '483s'. The other seven classes, totalling 235 engines, were rebuilt between 1904 and 1908 with 175 psi H class boilers and forty-four were subsequently fitted with G7 Belpaires between 1909 and 1912. It was from these H and G7 boilered locomotives that the '483' Class rebuilds were produced. The histories of the classes from which they were drawn were briefly as follows:

'1562' Class. Thirty locomotives numbered 1562–1581 and 1657–1666 were built at Derby in 1882 and 1883 to Order Nos. 370, 400 and 430. They had 140 psi B Class boilers, 18in cylinders with slide valves and 6ft 8½in driving wheels on an 8ft 6in coupled wheelbase. Between 1906 and 1908 they were rebuilt with H boilers and sixteen of them later received saturated G7 boilers with extended smokeboxes. In 1907 they became Nos. 328–357. Two of the H and three of the G7–boilered engines were rebuilt as '483s' by the LMS.

'1738' Class. These twenty engines were produced by Derby Works, ten to O/554 and the rest to O/615, as Nos. 1738–1757 in 1885 and 1886. As built they had higher pressure 160 psi B Class boilers, 18 in cylinders with slide valves and 7ft driving wheels on an 8ft 6in coupled wheelbase. Rebuilt with H boilers in 1906 and 1907, they became Nos. 358–377. Ten of them were later rebuilt again with saturated G7 boilers and extended smokeboxes. One of the H-boilered engines was rebuilt as a '483' by the Midland and the LMS dealt with another four.

'1808' Class. Derby Works turned out twenty-five engines numbered 1808–1822, 80–87, 11 and 14 to O/678, O/734 and O/920 in 1888 and 1891. Originally they had 160 psi B

Class boilers, slide valves, 18in cylinders and 6ft 6in coupled wheels on an 8ft 6in wheelbase. All were given H boilers in 1904 and 1905 and they were renumbered 378–402 in 1907. Sixteen later received saturated G7 boilers with extended smokeboxes. Two of the remaining nine were withdrawn still in H-boilered condition and the rest rebuilt as '483s', five by the Midland in 1922 and two by the LMS. A further ten locomotives with 18½in cylinders were produced by Beyer, Peacock to a similar design in 1900 as an extension to an order for the Midland & Great Northern Railway. In Midland documents they were referred to as 'like C, M&GN' and although some writers have called them the '2581' Class we regard them as '1808s'. Originally Nos. 2581–2590, they became 473–482 in 1907. All were rebuilt with H boilers in 1904 and 1905 and five were later rebuilt by the Midland as '483s'.

'2183' Class. Sharp, Stewart built twenty of these as Class L engines, numbered 2183–2202, in 1892 and Derby Works produced another five, Nos. 156–160, to O/1458 in 1896. They had the 9ft wheelbase necessary to accommodate the longer fireboxes of their 160 psi D Class boilers, 18½in cylinders with slide valves and 7ft

diameter coupled wheels. In 1907 they became Nos. 403–427. All were rebuilt with H boilers between 1906 and 1908 and then rebuilt as '483' Class engines by the Midland.

'2203' Class. Of these forty-five engines, fifteen were built by Sharp, Stewart as Class O in 1893 and the rest by Derby Works to O/1235, 1276 and 1410 in 1894 and 1895. The Sharp, Stewart locomotives were originally Nos. 2203–2217 and the others 184–199, 161–164 and 230–239. In 1907 they became Nos. 428–472. As built they had 160 psi D Class boilers, 18½in slide valve cylinders and 6ft 6in coupled wheels on a 9ft wheelbase. All received H boilers between 1904 and 1906. The Midland rebuilt twenty-six of them as '483s' and the LMS dealt with a further four after the Grouping.

'150' Class. Out of a total of forty locomotives, ten were renewals of the earlier '1667' Class that were produced by Derby Works to O/444 in 1884 as Nos. 1667–1676. As first built they had 140 psi B Class boilers with Joy valve gear driving slide valves to 19in cylinders and their 7ft diameter driving wheels were mounted on an 8ft 6in wheelbase. Between 1886 and 1888 higher pressure 160 psi B Class boilers were fitted, although some engines subsequently reverted to 140 psi ones. Beginning in October 1896, they were rebuilt with 160 psi D Class boilers, 19in cylinders, piston valves and 7ft coupled wheels on a 9ft wheelbase. Ten new locomotives to a closely similar design were built at Derby in 1897 to O/1597 as Nos. 150, 153–155 and 204–209. In 1899 Sharp, Stewart produced twenty R Class engines, numbered 2421–2440, which differed in having 18½in cylinders. Between 1906 and 1908 all received H boilers and fourteen of the Derby engines had their cylinder diameter reduced to 18½in. In 1907 the whole series became Nos. 483–522. Beginning in 1912 they were rebuilt, all except one with G7S boilers, which process was complete by the end of 1913. Two of them, Nos. 484 and 492, were different in that they initially had smaller cylinders and higher boiler pressures than the standard rebuilds, as described later, and 484 had a saturated G7 boiler from May 1913 to June 1914.

'60' Class. Thirty of these engines were built at Derby to O/1635, 1834 and 2041 between 1898 and 1901. Their numbers were 60–69, 93, 138, 139, 151, 152, 165–169, 805–809 and 2636–2640. Neilson, Reid & Co. produced another ten, numbered 2591–2600, as their Midland Class T in 1901. They were the largest of the Johnson 'slim boilered' 4-4-0s with 7ft diameter wheels on a 9ft 6in wheelbase. The latter dimension was occasioned by the use of 170 psi E Class boilers having longer fireboxes than those previously used. All had piston valves and the first sixteen Derby engines had 19½in cylinders; the rest had 19in ones. In 1907 they became Nos. 523–562. Between 1906 and 1908 all received H boilers and, starting in 1913, they were rebuilt as '483' Class engines, the last one being completed in 1915.

Quoted wheel diameters of locomotives before rebuilding are taken from Midland Railway specifications and may differ from those used elsewhere. As we have explained before, alterations in tyre thickness after about 1900 led to notional wheel sizes increasing by ½in, although the amount of wear and machining tolerated before tyres were replaced meant that actual in-service diameters could be considerably less.

The first of the '483' Class rebuilds was No. 494, which left Derby Works in February 1912. It started life in 1897 with a D Class boiler and had received an HX boiler less than 4½ years before being rebuilt in superheated form. How much of the original engine was left must be open to question but at least the coupled wheels were the same. A further 29 engines were rebuilt in 1912 including No. 483, which was completed in the November, and by the end of 1914 the total had reached 95. The LMS took 142 into stock and the last one, No. 364, was finished in January 1924. The order numbers for rebuilding roughly corresponded to their original classes as follows:

O/3942 dated 21st June 1911 – Nos. 483–522
O/4116 dated 29th July 1912 – Nos. 523–562
O/4311 dated 31st July 1913 – Nos. between 403 and 427
O/4476 dated 22nd April 1914 – Nos. 428–482
O/5664 dated 9th January 1922 – Nos. between 328 and 482

Numbers of the rebuilt engines were 332, 337, 351, 353, 356, 359, 362, 364, 370, 377, 394–397, 400–427, 430, 432–434, 436–439, 443, 444, 446–448, 450, 452–456, 458, 459, 461–464, 466, 468, 470–472, 477–480 and 482–562.

Although Deeley had left the Midland several years earlier, design features seen in his version of the Compound and in the '990' Class 4-4-0s were evident in the rebuilt engines. This was probably due mainly to the influence of the Chief Draughtsman at Derby, J.E. Anderson, who reputedly had more to do with the design than the CME, Henry Fowler. The vertical plate between buffer beam and platform, smokebox door fastened by dogs, parallel-sided and capuchoned chimney, cab with four front windows and contiguous rear splasher, and stepped platform had all been seen on the Deeley Compounds. The latter feature, designed to allow better access to the coupling rod ends for oiling should a rod be at the top of its travel, gave the engines a more attractive and puissant line.

Weight in working order of the locomotive was 53 tons 7 cwt 3 qtr of which 18 tons 18 cwt 2 qtr rested on the bogie, 17 tons 10 cwt on the leading coupled axle and 16 tons 19 cwt 1 qtr on the rear. A 3,250 gallon tender weighed a nominal 39 tons 16 cwt 3 qtr and a 3,500 gallon one 41 tons 4 cwt. Engine wheelbase was 6ft + 7ft 2½in + 9ft 6in and total length of locomotive and tender over the buffers was 54ft 3½in. In 1919 they were allocated to ED 69.

Boiler

The steel G7S boiler with Schmidt type superheater had been developed from the H via the G7 and was dimensionally the same as its forebears with precisely the same outer firebox as the G7.[8] The barrel was 10ft 5$^{15}/_{16}$in long (10ft 10⅝in between tubeplates) and 4ft 8in diameter outside the first ring. The firebox was 7ft long with a 21.1 sq ft grate. Inside the barrel were 148 tubes of 1¾in diameter and twenty-one 5⅛in superheater flues, which, with the superheater elements, gave a total heating surface of 1420 sq ft. This was slightly more than the H or G7 boilers.[9]

In keeping with Schmidt's theories of superheating, the pressure was reduced from the 175 psi of the H and G7 boilers to just 160 psi (there were two exceptions discussed later). To compensate for this, the cylinder diameter was increased to 20⅛in. Unfortunately, Schmidt's calculations were flawed, as he hadn't taken density into account, and this combination of pressure and cylinder size helped make the engines less efficient than they otherwise might have been. It is possible, however, that the lower pressure helped produce the low maintenance costs referred to later. Twin Ramsbottom safety valves and one lock-up valve were mounted on the firebox of the early rebuilds but it was decided that the lock-up valves were unnecessary so they were omitted on later boilers and removed from those that had them.

The smokebox was longer than the one on the H boiler and was similar to that used on the saturated G7 fitted to the '378' Class rebuilt 4—4—0s. It was fitted with a superheater

Once the superheater damper had been deleted, the separate handrail on the left-hand side of the smokebox was extended to join the front of the boiler handrail. As can be seen in this picture of No. 462, a 1916 rebuild, more bolt heads had appeared on the upper front frames by this time. The photograph gives an excellent idea of how the front end of the engine was painted. Although the smokebox door ring and hinges were polished steel, the dogs and the hinge attachments on the smokebox front were black. Close inspection shows that the bottom of the vacuum pipe standard was black, fine lined pale straw to match the lower edge of the buffer beam behind it. The tender was an unmodified 3,250 gallon one and it can be seen that the upper beading lined up well below the butt strip on the cab side. H. GORDON TIDEY

Photographed at Holbeck not long after being rebuilt in 1922, No. 477 was coupled to a modified 3,250 gallon tender of the type we describe as category 2. Note that it had coal rails ending at the front plate, built-in tool boxes and extended front coal plate but that the footsteps were still mounted directly on to the frames. On the locomotive, snap-headed rivets can be seen on the platform angle, footsteps and supports as well as the smokebox. On the front frames there were a large number of protruding bolt heads and so the Derby makers' plates were moved to the splasher sides. The lock-up safety valve was omitted and the casing for the bases of the twin Ramsbottom valves was circular. As with No. 551, seen at about the same time, the smokebox was all black and the coupling rod fluting was painted. REAL PHOTOGRAPHS

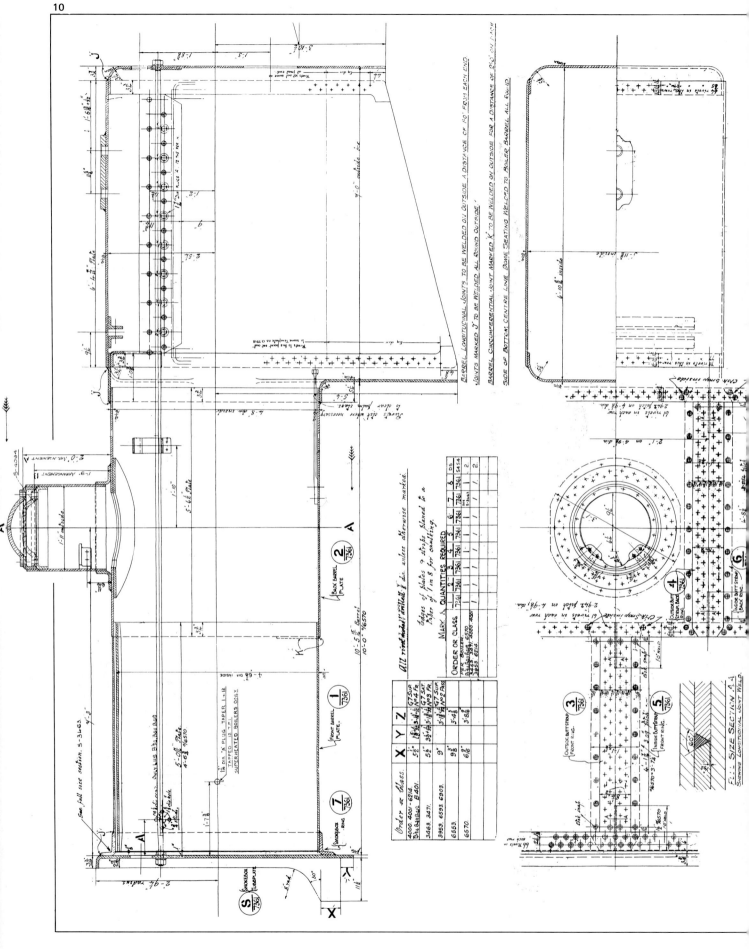

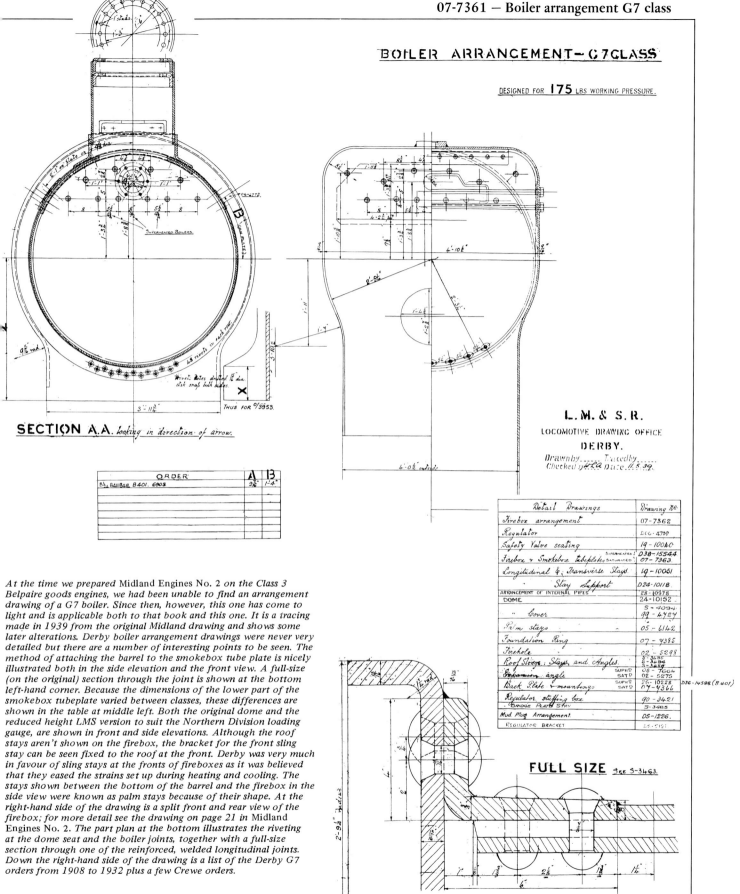

BOILER ARRANGEMENT — G7CLASS

DESIGNED FOR **175** LBS WORKING PRESSURE.

SECTION A.A. *looking in direction of arrow.*

L. M. & S. R.
LOCOMOTIVE DRAWING OFFICE
DERBY.

FULL SIZE See S-3463.

DO7-7361

Detail Drawings	Drawing №
Firebox arrangement	07-7362
Regulator	DCG-4739
Safety Valve seating	19-100A0
Firebox & Smokebox tubeplates SUPERHEATED / SATURATED	D38-15544 / 07-7363
Longitudinal & Transverse Stays	19-10051
" Stay Support	D24-10118
ARRANGEMENT OF INTERNAL PIPES	28-10978
DOME	24-10152
" Cover	S-4094
" "	99-4727
Palm stays	05-6142
Foundation Ring	07-4385
Firehole	02-5298
Roof Slings; Stays, and Angles.	S-3086 / S-3484 / S-3489
Expansion angle SUPH / SAT	08-7664 / 02-5275
Back Plate & mountings SUPH / SAT	26-10228 / 07-4366
Regulator stuffing box	90-3421
BRIDGE PLATE STAY	S-3485
Mud Plug Arrangement	DS-1226
REGULATOR BRACKET	LS-5121

D36-14588(B401)

At the time we prepared Midland Engines No. 2 on the Class 3 Belpaire goods engines, we had been unable to find an arrangement drawing of a G7 boiler. Since then, however, this one has come to light and is applicable both to that book and this one. It is a tracing made in 1939 from the original Midland drawing and shows some later alterations. Derby boiler arrangement drawings were never very detailed but there are a number of interesting points to be seen. The method of attaching the barrel to the smokebox tube plate is nicely illustrated both in the side elevation and the front view. A full-size (on the original) section through the joint is shown at the bottom left-hand corner. Because the dimensions of the lower part of the smokebox tubeplate varied between classes, these differences are shown in the table at middle left. Both the original dome and the reduced height LMS version to suit the Northern Division loading gauge, are shown in front and side elevations. Although the roof stays aren't shown on the firebox, the bracket for the front sling stay can be seen fixed to the roof at the front. Derby was very much in favour of sling stays at the fronts of fireboxes as it was believed that they eased the strains set up during heating and cooling. The stays shown between the bottom of the barrel and the firebox in the side view were known as palm stays because of their shape. At the right-hand side of the drawing is a split front and rear view of the firebox; for more detail see the drawing on page 21 in Midland Engines No. 2. The part plan at the bottom illustrates the riveting at the dome seat and the boiler joints, together with a full-size section through one of the reinforced, welded longitudinal joints. Down the right-hand side of the drawing is a list of the Derby G7 orders from 1908 to 1932 plus a few Crewe orders.

ORDER		A	B
B½, B411 B412 B401. 6903		9½"	1'-4"

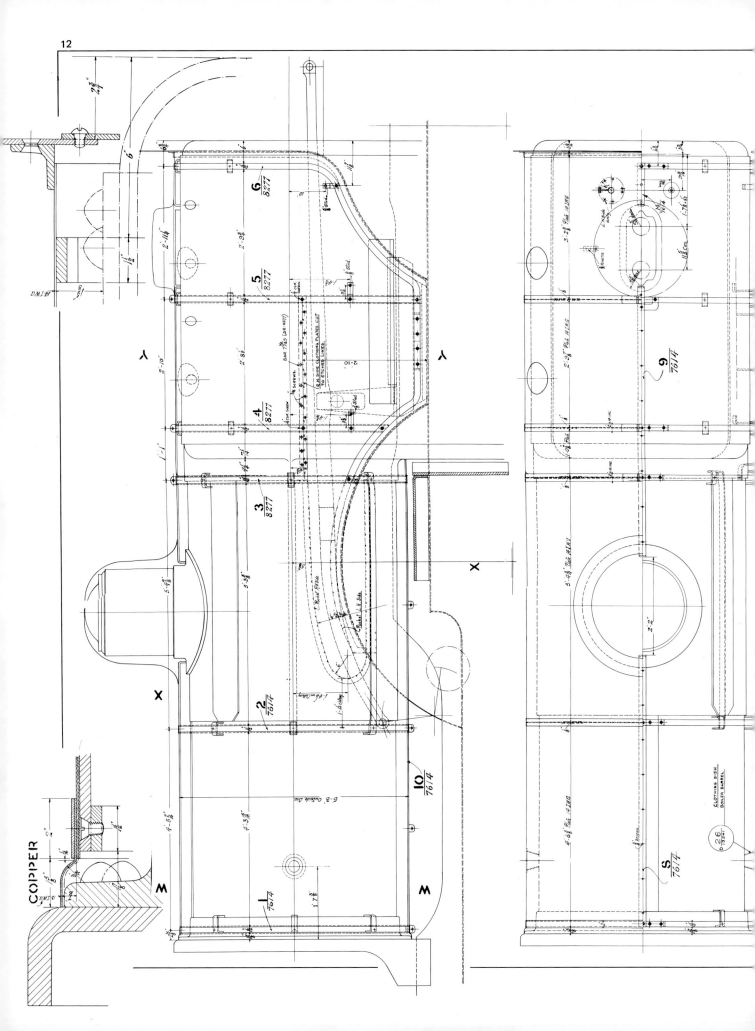

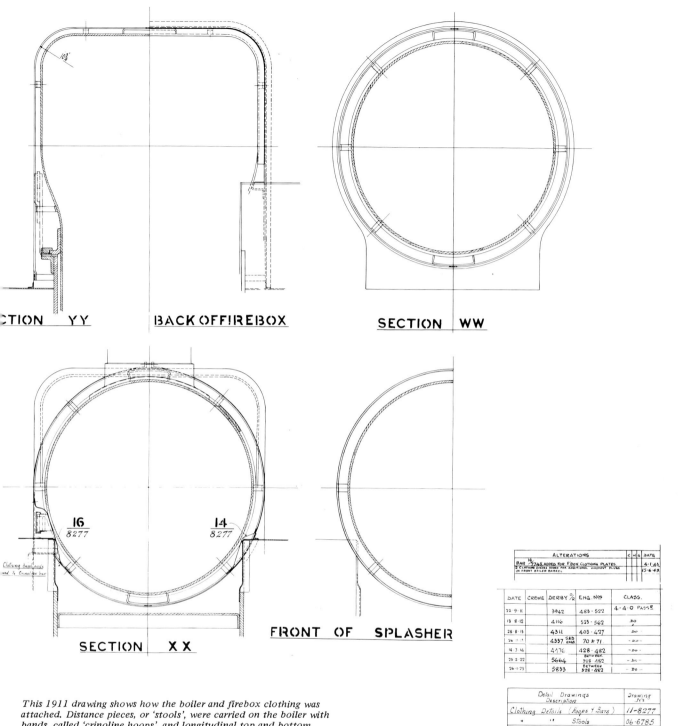

CTION Y Y   BACK OF FIREBOX   SECTION WW

16
8277

14
8277

SECTION X X   FRONT OF SPLASHER

ALTERATIONS		C	H	G	DATE
BAR 16 77AS ADDED FOR F BOX CLOTHING PLATES					4·1·43
2 CLOTHING DISHES ADDED FOR ADDITIONAL WASHOUT PLUGS IN FRONT BOILER BARREL					15·6·49

DATE	CREWE	DERBY ⁰/₂	ENG.Nᵒˢ	CLASS.
22·9·11		3942	483 - 522	4·4·0 PASSᴳ
13·8·12		4116	523 - 562	DO
28·8·13		4311	403 - 427	DO
26·1·14		4337 S&D ENGS	70 & 71	- DO -
14·7·14		4476	428 - 482	- DO -
23·2·22		5664	BETWEEN 328-482	- DO -
26·1·23		5833	BETWEEN 328-482	- DO -

Detail Drawings Description	Drawing Nᵒˢ
Clothing Details (Hoops & Bars)	11-8277
" " Stools	06-6785
Dome Cover	00-4755
Safety Valve Casing	21-9470
Lugs for Clothing Bands	5-494
Casing for Washout Plugs	D-13241

This 1911 drawing shows how the boiler and firebox clothing was attached. Distance pieces, or 'stools', were carried on the boiler with bands, called 'crinoline hoops', and longitudinal top and bottom bars attached to them by countersunk screws. Lagging was silicate cotton covered with thin zinc sheets and the clothing was 14 iwg steel held in place by 2in wide bands of the same material over the transverse joints. A shaped copper fairing, held in place by the front band, covered the smokebox angle. There were recesses, or pockets, in the clothing to clear the splasher on the left-hand side and both splasher and reversing rod on the right, as marked on the side elevation. At the top of the drawing are full-size (on the original) sections through the joints between boiler clothing and smokebox and between firebox clothing and cab front. At either side are cross-sections at various points. Top left is a section at the front ring just behind the smokebox with one taken at the front of the driving splasher below it. At the bottom right is another on the mid point

of the driving splasher whilst above that is a split section, to the left of the centreline, being between the driving and trailing splashers and to the right at the rear of the firebox. The six detail drawings accompanying the arrangement are listed at the bottom. Later alterations were the addition in 1943 of the position of the side bars on the firebox and details of the dishes for the washout plugs on the front boiler ring in 1949. The dome and casing shown on the drawing are the original, tall types.

damper in keeping with early thinking on protecting superheater elements from being damaged when there was no steam passing through them. There were two ways in which Midland superheater dampers could be made to operate depending on the driver's selection. If it was desired to prevent hot gases from passing through the flues when the regulator was shut, the control valve was set to leave the damper closed unless the main steam pipe from the regulator had steam pressure in it. When working trains with frequent stops, the control valve could be set to keep the damper open irrespective of the regulator position unless the blower was turned on, when it would shut. The control valve was on the left-hand side of the smokebox. After a while the Locomotive Department realised that the gases in the superheater flues were not, in fact, hot enough to cause any damage to the elements, even when they had no steam passing through them, and that the dampers were an unnecessary, costly and troublesome complication. After about 1916 they were omitted from further rebuilds and removed from those engines that had them. Superheater headers were originally cast-steel but trouble was experienced in producing castings of high enough quality and so cast-iron later became the standard material. The first G7S-boilered engines were provided with flush-riveted smokeboxes but soon snap-headed rivets began to appear on them.

As rebuilt the engines had two Gresham & Craven live-steam under-type injectors mounted on the step plates. After the fitting of Davies & Metcalfe exhaust steam injectors to the 'Royal Scots' had indicated that worthwhile fuel savings were possible, it was decided to equip many more LMS locomotives with them. Approval was given in May 1931 for all the '483s' to be modified and O/7924 was issued in the July, detailing the work that began soon afterwards authorised by NWO 2446. In April 1937, however, Stanier wrote, 'Due to the introduction of larger types of engines for working the more important passenger and freight services, it is considered that the provision of this fitting does not afford

the savings previously anticipated.' Existing stocks of injectors were used up but no more were ordered. The majority of the class were modified and we can confirm the following engines as having them: Nos. 332, 351, 353, 356, 359, 370, 377, 394–6, 400–4, 406, 407, 409–19, 421, 424–7, 432, 434, 437, 438, 443, 448, 450, 452–6, 458, 461–3, 468, 470–2, 477–9, 483, 484, 486, 487, 489, 493–8, 500–5, 507, 509, 512–15, 518–22, 524–9, 531–7, 539, 540, 543–552, 554, 556, 558 and 559. Because we have found the engine history cards to be somewhat suspect in certain areas, however, we cannot state with any certainty that none of the remainder had them. From photographic evidence we know of some that definitely retained their left-hand live-steam injectors. They were Nos. 337, 362, 397, 405, 420, 436, 439, 444, 447, 464, 480, 482, 491, 499, 511, 538, 541, 553, 557 and 562. Thus there were twenty-four about which we are uncertain.

Exhaust injector-fitted locomotives could be identified by the elbow-shaped steam pipe coming out of the left-hand side of the smokebox, through the platform and behind the coupled wheels below ashpan level to the injector mounted under the left-hand side of the cab. Part-way along this pipe was a grease separator. This was necessary to prevent oil, which was picked up from the cylinders by the steam and held in suspension, from getting into the injector cones or back into the boiler. If it got into the cones it could form a coating and cause the injector to stop. In the boiler it would lead to the formation of sludge. Inside the inlet to the separator was a fixed vane that imparted a swirling motion to the steam. The suspended oil was flung against the side of the casing and the steam continued via a more restricted exit. The oil then collected in the bottom of the casing where an automatic drip valve allowed it to escape. At the bottom of the body of the injector was a water strainer. During the severe winter of 1939–40, difficulties were experienced with the injectors freezing up and so drain cocks were fitted to the strainers. This minor job (the cocks cost 2/5d each) was not reported as complete until February 1947.

Deeley-pattern sliding fire doors were specified in the drawing lists for the first four orders for rebuilding but O/5644 reverted to the Johnson double-flap type. Later G7S boilers built for LMS standard 4F and 2P locomotives, however, had a different design of sliding fire doors and, since the boilers were interchangeable, some of them found their way onto '483s'.[10] It is possible that some boilers were also altered when they were repaired and so the question of which engines had which type and when is extremely complex. Both flap and sliding-type doors were in evidence after nationalisation but we are unable to say whether the latter included any of the Deeley-pattern ones. Beginning in 1942, the design of the brick arch was altered to use standard bricks and thus reduce the number of different types held in stock.

Under the boiler and firebox clothing was the normal Midland silicate cotton insulation covered by thin zinc sheets. In about 1940 this system was replaced by asbestos mattresses. The original fireboxes on the '483s' had washout doors on the shoulders, but from about 1928 fireboxes on new G7S boilers began to be fitted with a row of washout plugs along each side above the handrail. Some fireboxes had single washout plugs further down and single plugs were also sometimes fitted each side of the first ring of the boiler barrel below the handrail. When an engine underwent a boiler change it retained its clothing, i.e., the clothing stayed with the engine rather than the boiler. Therefore, if the new boiler had washout plugs, holes for them would have to be cut in the panels but, if a subsequently fitted boiler had shoulder-mounted doors, they would become redundant. Thus locomotives could gradually receive a 'full set' of openings, only some of which would be required at any particular time. If washout doors were present, the covers on the shoulders of the firebox had prominent fastenings in the centre; otherwise blanking plates were fitted with four fixing screws. The presence of washout plugs was denoted by the holes in the clothing being uncovered. Cover plates indicated that there were no plugs beneath.

12-8403 — Smokebox arrangement G7 rebuilds with 'Midland' superheater

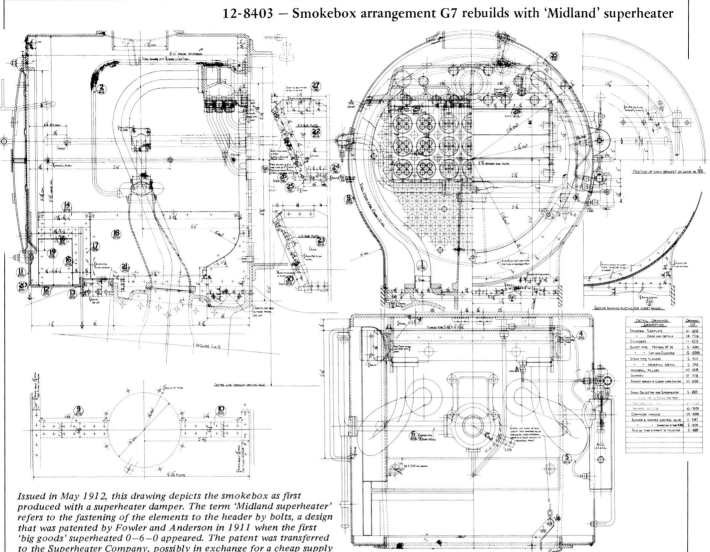

DETAIL DRAWINGS	
DESCRIPTION	DRAWING Nº
SMOKEBOX TUBEPLATE	10 · 6/22
DOOR AND DETAILS	08 · 77/8
CYLINDERS	11 · 82/3
BLAST PIPE PATTERN Nº 34	6 · 1680
CAP AND BLOWER	12 · 6398
STEAM PIPE FLANGES	6 · 1510
ORDERING SKETCH	6 · 1746
HANDRAIL PILLARS	09 · 5074
CHIMNEY	07 · 7078
EXHAUST BRANCH & ELBOW-LARGE EJECTOR	10 · 6130
STEAM COLLECTOR FOR SUPERHEATER	6 · 1405
	07 · 7037
DAMPER DETAILS	10 · 7079
COMMODE HANDLE	05 · 4266
BLOWER & DAMPER CONTROL VALVE	11 · 8167
CONNECTION TO TANK FLANGE	5 · 6743
STUD ON TUBE ELEMENT TO COLLECTOR	6 · 1485

Issued in May 1912, this drawing depicts the smokebox as first produced with a superheater damper. The term 'Midland superheater' refers to the fastening of the elements to the header by bolts, a design that was patented by Fowler and Anderson in 1911 when the first 'big goods' superheated 0–6–0 appeared. The patent was transferred to the Superheater Company, possibly in exchange for a cheap supply of elements to Derby Works, at the same time as this drawing was issued. In some respects the drawing is not as detailed as some smokebox arrangements, e.g. the G7 0–6–0s, although the layout of the tubeplate is more so. At the top left is a side elevation of the smokebox cut in half with a part plan below it showing the butt strips at the joint. To the right of that is a sectional plan, with the smokebox door at the bottom, and there is a split front view above it. To the right of the centreline the bottom half shows an external view, with some internal details chain dotted, whilst above it the front plate and door have been removed and we are looking inside the smokebox. The left-hand side shows a section but, as with other arrangements, there are various sectional planes through blastpipe and superheater header. Between side and front views are details of the mounting plates for the superheater damper. When the smokebox door was opened, a chain attached to it opened the damper. The chain attachment bracket on the door is shown at the top right-hand corner, as well as on the plan view, and below it are details of the gusset angles where the front, cylindrical part of the smokebox joined the main portion. Basically, the steam circuit was as follows. When the regulator in the dome was opened, saturated steam was allowed into a pipe that carried it to the superheater header. This pipe was the large-bore one shown in the middle of the header on the cross-section. The steam then passed through the superheater elements, which were U-shaped return pipes mounted in pairs inside the flues, where it was subjected to further heating. The flues and elements are shown in three rows in the upper part of the tubeplate on the cross-section and on the side elevation of the GA. Superheated steam then passed through the two steel pipes running from the header, round the inside of the smokebox wrapper, down into the steam chest and through the valves into the cylinders. Once it had done its work in the cylinders, it was

exhausted through the blastpipe and out of the chimney. The convergent shape of the blastpipe accelerated the exhaust and reduced its pressure. Thus, as it passed through the smokebox on its way to the chimney, it drew gases through the tubes from the fire to heat the boiler water. So that the flow of gases through the small tubes would be maintained when the regulator was closed, a blower was fitted. This enabled the driver to direct live steam into an annular chamber around the top of the blastpipe, whence it would issue from a circle of holes up to the chimney and continue to draw the hot gases forward. The blower pipe, annotated as item 2 on the side elevation, can be seen entering the smokebox at the top rear and feeding into the front of the blower ring. Note the support bracket next to the base of the chimney. Details of the galleries within the ring and the exhaust holes in the top have been omitted from this drawing but can be seen in the G7 smokebox arrangement in Midland Engines No. 2. *Also entering the top of the blastpipe from the right-hand side (left-hand side of the drawing) is the large ejector exhaust. (Due to a typographical error in* Midland Engines No. 2, *a few lines were missed out with the result that the ejector exhaust became referred to as the blower.) Although the drawing is dated 1912, it shows a later arrangement of the ejector exhaust pipe than that on the GA. Operation of the superheater damper is described in the text. It is shown on both cross-section and plan, mounted on the left-hand side of the smokebox, which is the right-hand side of the drawing. The lower part of the external mechanism is the control valve, whilst above it is the operating cylinder. The three damper doors, item 28 on the cross-section, closed off the flues and so prevented hot gases being drawn along them. The 18 drawings and sketches that were used in conjunction with the smokebox arrangement are listed at the lower right.*

Since the layout changed depending on the type of firebox with which a locomotive was fitted, only reference to photographs can indicate what the situation was for a particular engine at a particular time. From photographic evidence it would appear that the most common arrangement in BR days was for upper washout plugs to be present with covers fitted over the lower holes and blanking plates on the shoulders, although other combinations were evident. We believe that the fireboxes on some G7S boilers had both washout doors on the shoulders and plugs along the sides, but we have no evidence of which engines were fitted with them or when.

The bases of the safety valves were covered by an oval casing that stretched back almost to the spectacle plate. Even when the lock-up

valve was omitted, the same type of cover was used until a circular version appeared on the last few engines to be rebuilt. Under LMS ownership the Ramsbottom valves were steadily replaced by 'pop' valves.

The original dome casings gave the engines an overall height from the rails of 13ft 3in. When the LMS version of the '483', the standard Class 2P, was introduced in 1928, this was reduced to a nominal 12ft 10⅝in (referred to in later documents as a more realistic 12ft 11in) for the more restrictive Northern Division routes. A lower dome and a much shorter, flatter-topped casing were used. Because most G7S boilers were freely interchangeable between the '483s' and LMS-built 2Ps, as well as the 0–6–4 passenger tank engines and both Midland and LMS built 4Fs (which also included low-domed ver-

sions), some '483s' started to appear a few years later with low domes and casings.[10] A shorter version of the Deeley capuchon chimney had also been introduced for the same reason and again engines could be seen with either type. Even when the Stanier chimneys without capuchons were introduced in late 1936 there were two different heights and gradually the situation became very complex. Locomotives were to be seen with long chimneys and low domes or any other combination that could exist. It was even found that there were engines with low domes but tall casings over them. An attempt was made in 1939 to sort the situation out but it was never really successful and various combinations were always evident. Locomotives with long chimneys or tall domes were not supposed to work over the Northern

We have included this undated picture of an unidentified Class 2 engine, which displays Midland livery, in order to show what lay beneath the boiler clothing. The locomotive had been involved in an accident and we can see the extent of the damage. The crinoline hoops and stools that held the clothing clear of the boiler and created a gap into which the silicate cotton was placed, can be clearly seen.   COLLECTION R. J. ESSERY

Even more snap-head rivets appeared on the '483s' following repairs in the 1930s. In August 1939 No. 337 was photographed at Derby with them all around its splasher and cabside beading and angles. Although its boiler was without side washout plugs, it had received holes in the clothing for access to the plugs on a previous boiler. Since they were unnecessary at the time it was photographed, they were covered. The one between hand-rail and platform, however, wasn't. Note that rain gutters had by this time been welded on to the eaves of the cab. Chimney and dome casing were long and tall Deeley types. The freshly applied livery was the final LMS style of lined black with yellow shaded vermilion scroll and serif letters and numbers. The tender was a category 3 with built-in toolboxes and separate footstep supports but short sides. COLLECTION R. J. ESSERY

Division and some other branch lines, this fact being indicated by a blue disc painted on the cab side (see livery section). Stanier-pattern chimneys gradually replaced the Deeley type.

To try to reduce the concentration of dissolved salts that caused scale in the boiler, a system called continuous blow-down was adopted that allowed a small quantity of water to drain from the boiler whenever the regulator was open. On the LMS it was first fitted to the taper-boiler types, then, in March 1936, an instruction was issued to fit it to over 4,000 other LMS locomotives including the '483s'. On tank engines the water was discharged into the ashpan but tender locomotives had it taken through a cooling coil in the tender tank before it was discharged underneath the buffer beam just inside the right-hand rail. The PW Department, however, didn't like hot water being poured onto the track as it caused corrosion of the rails and chairs and damage to the sleepers, especially in tunnels. Eventually, after strong representations from the Civil Engineer, it was decided in 1950 that the discharge on all locomotives should be into the ashpan. The alteration was unpopular with many footplatemen as the steam produced could drift up the sides of the firebox and obscure the view from the cab as well as leading to condensation in the cab itself.

Cylinders and Motion

The new $20\frac{1}{2}$in cylinders were designed on the basis of Schmidt's erroneous calculations referred to previously. It is possible that suspicions about the boiler pressure and cylinder diameter were entertained at an early stage because No. 489 was rebuilt in April 1913 with $19\frac{1}{2}$in cylinders and a 175 psi G7S boiler. A month later No. 484 was rebuilt with $19\frac{1}{2}$in cylinders and a saturated G7 boiler. Presumably this was for comparison with the 'standard' $20\frac{1}{2}$in cylinder/160 psi superheated arrangement but, if so, the results don't seem to have justified immediate alteration to the design. In June 1914 No. 484 received a 160 psi G7S and $20\frac{1}{2}$in cylinders and 489 followed suit a year later. It is possible, of course, that the war was a factor in cancelling any thoughts of altering the class as a whole. The idea of using smaller cylinders was resurrected in 1922 and a sketch was added to the drawing lists for O/3942 and O/4476 in December giving details of lining them to $19\frac{1}{2}$in, the latter being annotated '5 engines only'. Nothing further seems to have been done in

Midland days and the only evidence we can find of the modification being carried out, which comes from the locomotive register, relates to three of the O/3942 locomotives after the Grouping. Nos. 502, 509 and 522 were altered in January 1927, April 1926 and May 1928 respectively, all retaining 160 psi boilers. Whether this was a trial to assess the effectiveness of modifying the class as a whole or to do with the introduction of the LMS standard 2Ps with 180 psi boilers and 19in cylinders we don't know.

The 8in piston valves were rather small, short travel and mounted underneath the cylinders, which necessitated fairly tortuous steam passages.[11] All in all, the front end design was not conducive to the free flow of steam and, as a result, the performance of the engines was never as good as it might have been. As built, the piston valves had single Schmidt-type broad cast-iron rings. These devices could be as bad in the long term for locomotive performance as the Schmidt superheaters were beneficial. The single, broad rings were inflexible and as wear developed in the liners, steam leakage past them became excessive. After new locomotives had been fitted with multiple, thin rings that proved to be a vast improvement, consideration was

11-8241 – Motion arrangement

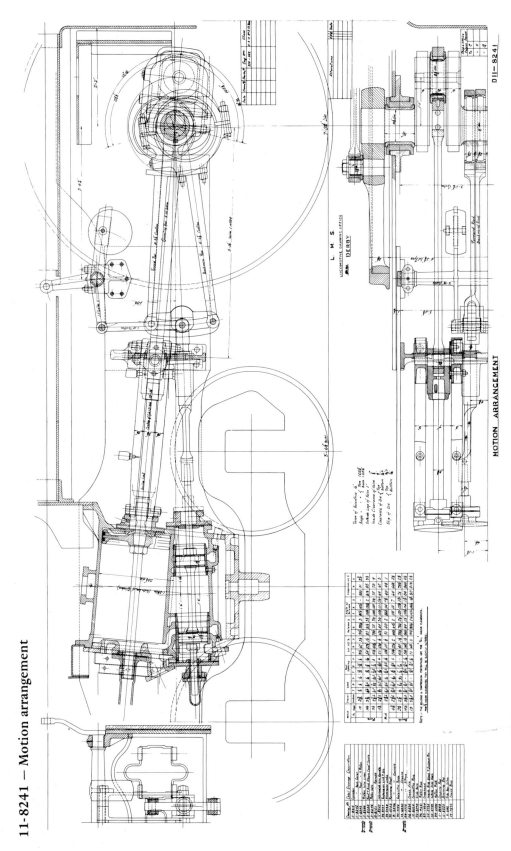

This drawing was issued to the shops for the production of locomotives to O/3942 on 2nd August 1911. Apart from the right-hand cylinder and motion arrangement, the side elevation also shows a section through the right-hand cylinder and piston valve. The plan has sections through the motion plate, crosshead, coupling rod end and bush, driving wheel, axlebox guides, axlebox, big end and eccentric straps. The principle of Stephenson valve gear is that the motion of each valve is derived from two eccentrics on one of the coupled axles. These eccentrics are connected to rods, seen marked 'forward' and 'backward' on the side elevation and at the bottom of the plan, which are pinned to either end of the curved, slotted expansion link between the driving and rear bogie wheels. Into the slot fits a sliding die block that is attached to the rear end of the intermediate valve spindle, which mates at its front end with the valve spindle itself. As the axle rotates, the eccentrics and rods convert the motion to fore and aft movement of the extremities of the expansion link. As drawn, this would result in insufficient movement of the valve spindle to open one of the ports and allow steam into the

cylinder as the motion is in mid-gear, or neutral, and the die block is at the fulcrum point of the expansion link (there would be some slight movement depending on the lap and lead of the valve but the principle remains). If the reversing shaft were to be moved forwards, however, the arm on the reversing shaft would rotate anti-clockwise and the lifting link would lower the expansion link so that the die block moved nearer to the top of the slot. This would bring the valve spindle more under the influence of the forward eccentric and increase its travel, closing one exhaust port and opening the other admission port so that steam was admitted to one end of the cylinder and power developed. The closer the die block got to the end of the lifting link, the greater the valve travel and the longer the admission port would be open. At the limit of downward movement of the lifting link, the engine would be in full forward gear and as the reversing rod was brought backwards, or 'notched up', the cut-off of steam admission would be reduced as a percentage of the stroke. Once past the mid-gear point, the engine would be in reverse.

No. 437 was photographed undergoing a general repair in No. 3 bay of 8 Shop at Derby. This picture shows double-flap type fire doors, lock-up safety valve, tall dome, and snap-headed rivets are evident on the upper footsteps and platform angle. Note the horn-keeps with horizontal retaining pins and the fact that the engine had yet to be fitted with an exhaust steam injector.
COLLECTION
R. J. ESSERY

given to replacing the Schmidt rings on older types. This widespread adoption of multiple rings was way overdue when the LMS decided in 1930 to fit the Compounds, S&DJR 2–8–0s and the Lickey banker with them.[12] In June 1931 the '483s' were included in the replacement programme, O/7972 being issued to cover the first twenty under the authority of NWO 2447. The new valves had four rings and were fitted when examinations called for the old ones to be changed. We presume that all the engines were eventually fitted with them, but the engine history cards are a bit inconsistent in recording the work done.

Whereas vertically-mounted slide valves would fall off their faces when steam was shut off, thus preventing a partial vacuum developing in the cylinders, piston valves maintained their seal. If such a partial vacuum was allowed to develop, hot gases and smokebox rubbish could be drawn into the cylinders with obvious detriment to the lubrication and the bores. Most designers simply provided anti-vacuum, air relief or 'snifting', valves on the saturated steam

side of the superheater header. The Midland, however, used Fowler-Anderson bypass valves that allowed communication between the two ends of the cylinder when steam pressure was reduced. These could be seen on the '483s' below the platform angle between the bogie wheels. Commencing in 1917, however, Midland piston valve engines were also fitted with air relief valves, although it wasn't until after 1920 that the later '483' rebuilds got them. The bypass valves could be a nuisance in service as failure of them would effectively stop a locomotive, and in the mid-1930s removal began. All of them were eventually taken off and air relief valves fitted to those engines that didn't already have them but, again, we can't give a date when the job was completed.

Inside Stephenson motion drove the valves. Some items were recovered from the old engines, e.g., crossheads, slidebars, piston rods, expansion links, valve spindles and reversing shafts, but not all those listed applied to all engines. Otherwise the motion was new.

Frames and Bogie
The one-inch thick steel frames were new and the coupled wheelbase was the familiar 9ft 6in used on the '60' Class and carried on in both the Compounds and '990s', although forward of the leading coupled axle they were nearly 2ft shorter than the Class 4 locomotives. The longitudinal dimensions were the same as the '60' Class, which enabled more parts to be re-used on them than on the other rebuilds. Engines from other classes were 2in longer between the leading coupled axle and the bogie in their rebuilt form than they had previously been. Each main frame was in two pieces, the lap joints stretching from the motion bracket back to a point just behind the weighshaft bearings, with 3/16in thick plates sandwiched between them. The rear portions were spaced 4ft 2⅛in apart and the forward ones 3ft 11¼in. The reduced width ahead of the joints enabled the rear bogie wheels to move laterally without large cut-outs in the frames. To accommodate the swing of the bogie, the front frames were angled inwards from a point just behind the leading bogie axleboxes to a spacing

11-8199 Frame arrangement *The caption to this drawing appears on page 22.*

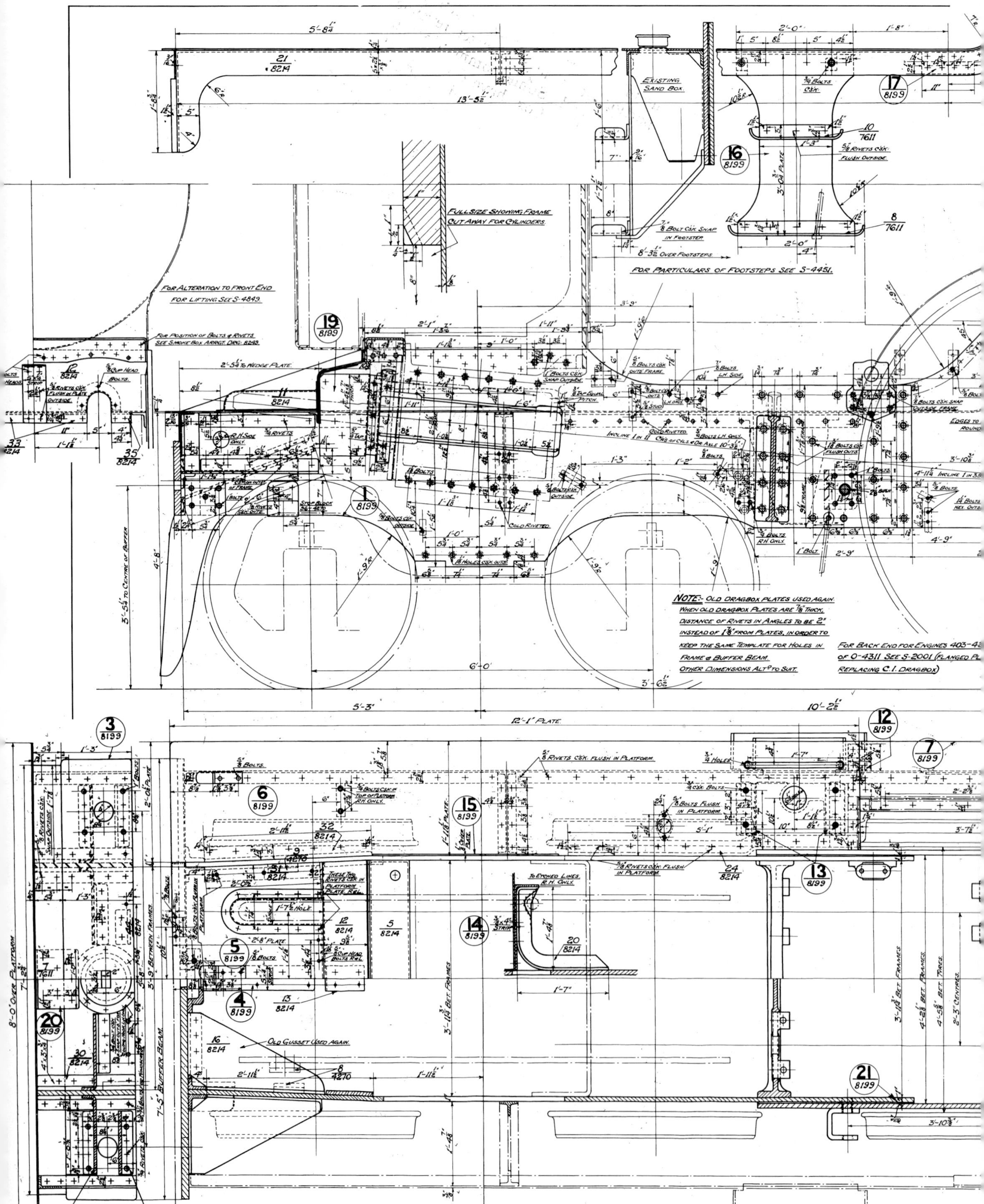

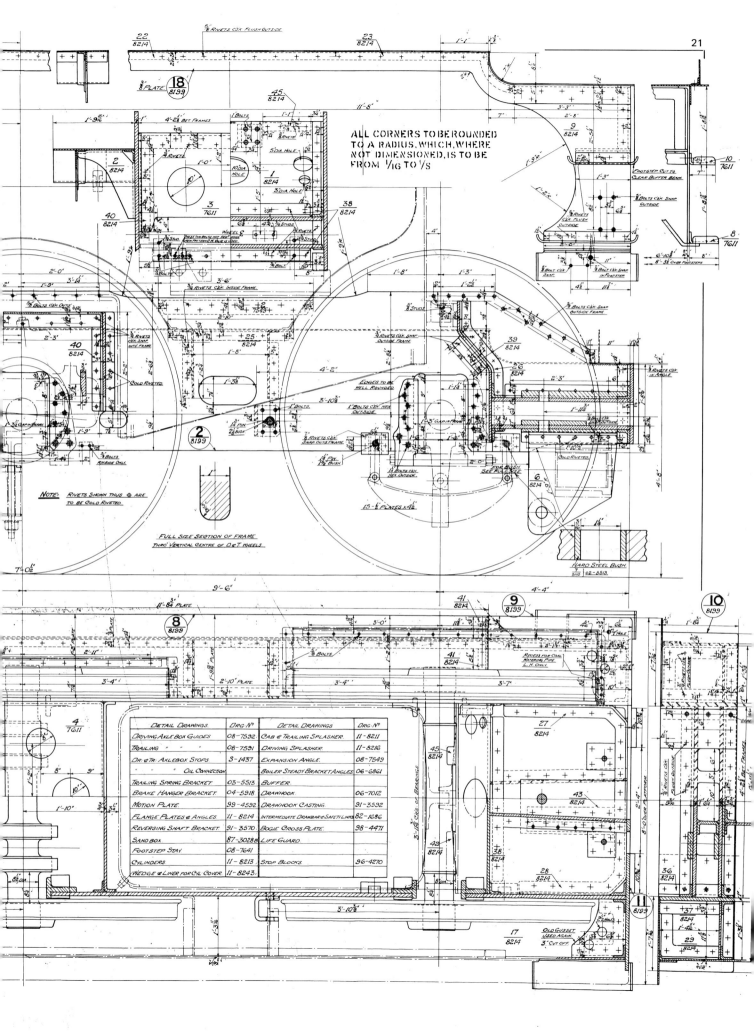

ALL CORNERS TO BE ROUNDED
TO A RADIUS, WHICH, WHERE
NOT DIMENSIONED, IS TO BE
FROM 1/16 TO 1/8

NOTE: RIVETS SHOWN THUS ⊕ ARE
TO BE COLD RIVETED.

FULL SIZE SECTION OF FRAME
THRO' VERTICAL CENTRE OF D. & T. WHEELS.

21

DETAIL DRAWINGS.	DRG. Nº	DETAIL DRAWINGS	DRG. Nº
DRIVING AXLE BOX GUIDES	08-7592	CAB & TRAILING SPLASHER	11-8211
TRAILING	08-7591	DRIVING SPLASHER	11-8216
DR. & TR. AXLEBOX STOPS	S-1437	EXPANSION ANGLE	08-7549
OIL CONNECTION		BOILER STEADY BRACKET ANGLES	06-6861
TRAILING SPRING BRACKET	03-5513	BUFFER	
BRAKE HANGER BRACKET	04-5918	DRAWHOOK	06-7012
MOTION PLATE	99-4592	DRAWHOOK CASTING	91-3592
FLANGE PLATES & ANGLES	11-8214	INTERMEDIATE DRAWBAR & SAFETY LINKS	82-4686
REVERSING SHAFT BRACKET	91-3570	BOGIE CROSS PLATE	98-4471
SAND BOX	87-3028B	LIFE GUARD	
FOOTSTEP STAY	08-7641	STOP BLOCKS	96-4270
CYLINDERS	11-8213		
WEDGE & LINER FOR OIL COVER	11-8243		

Buxton's No. 462 is seen here at Millhouses in September 1930 when prepared for its next turn of duty. Note the well-filled tender and the slaking pipe hooked around the horizontal cabside handrail. It was more common to allow it to hang down between 'the uprights', a railwayman's description of the two vertical handrails, one on the engine, the other on the tender. The locomotive appears in typical condition for this class during the mid-1930s when they were regularly employed upon local passenger trains, mostly on the Midland Division. PHOTOMATIC

11-8199 — Frame arrangement

This drawing shows the frame arrangement for the '483' Class rebuilds. Note that the twenty Sharp, Stewart L Class engines, Nos. 403-422, rebuilt to O/4311 had, as explained in the text, slightly different hind ends to the frames. This was due to the design of flanged plates used to replace the original cast-iron dragboxes. Along the top of the drawing is a side elevation of the platform angle, or outside frame as the Midland termed it, with a cross-section taken through the frame showing an end view of the sandbox and leading footstep. At the far right is a part section through the platform and cab side giving an end view of the footstep plate and steps. A section through the rear footsteps, support, stay, angle and cab side is at the right-hand side. As we have seen before with the 0-4-4 passenger tanks and the Class 3 Belpaire goods engines, the modified, extended footsteps as drawn were not generally fitted to superheater Class 2 engines, the simpler alternative of turning up the corners to provide a better foothold being used. The side elevation of the main frames shows that as well as having different springing arrangements, the leading and trailing coupled wheels also had different axlebox guides, although both had keeps with horizontal retaining pins. To the left of the side elevation is a part view looking forwards from just in front of the cylinders. Above the cylinder is a full-size (on the original) section through the frame showing how it was chamfered to accommodate the cylinder casting. Above the coupled wheels is a split cross-section. To the left of the centreline inside the frame is a section taken just forward of the large slot in the frame looking forward to the bracket supporting the raised platform and to the stretcher in front of the firebox. To the right is another section through the front portion of the dragbox looking forwards to the platework carrying the firebox steadying bracket. Below the frame and between the coupled wheels is a full-size section through the frame at the horns and to the right is one through one of the hardened steel bushes for the rear spring links. The upper half of the plan shows a view from above the platform and frame plate whilst the lower is a section below the level of the platform. The lapped joint between front and rear frames is readily apparent, as is the tapered-in front end. Positions of the bolts that held the frame plates together are shown on the side elevation. To the left of the plan is a split view of the buffer beam shown from the front above the centreline and the rear below it. To the right is a rear view of the hind buffer beam above the centreline and a section through the dragbox below. In the firebox space on the plan is a list of the 24 detail drawings that went with

the frame arrangement and at bottom right are notes relating to alterations incorporated between 1937 and 1942 that included removal of the bypass valves and modifications to the crank axle.

12-8372 — General arrangement 4—4—0 rebuilt passenger engine

This drawing shows the general arrangement of the first superheated Class 2 rebuilds to O/3942, Nos. 483-522, with a superheater damper and three safety valves. As we have written before, GAs varied depending on when, where and by whom they were drawn and interpretation can be difficult. The side elevation is as though the engine has been sectioned and we are looking through the structure towards the outside. Although much of this view is a half section on the centreline of the engine, there are components, such as the cylinders and valves, that are sectioned on different vertical planes. Some details, such as many of the boiler tubes, superheater elements and flues, have been omitted for clarity, although some of them are shown. The plan is in two portions. Below the centreline is a view from above the platform with the boiler, firebox clothing and cab removed and hidden details below the platform shown chain dotted. Above the centreline of the engine is a series of sections through components below the platform. There is, however, no common plane on which the sections are taken. Sections through the buffers, bogie, coupled wheels, motion and firebox are all taken on different planes whilst some items, such as the motion balance weights and brake rigging, are not sectioned and others, e.g. the cylinders, are not shown at all. Actual construction of the locomotives would have been undertaken using a series of detail and sub-structure arrangement drawings, some of which we have included. The overall GA was just to illustrate how it all went together. Points to note include the cylinder relief valves, one of which is shown at the lower front of the cylinder in the side elevation, which were fitted to prevent trapped water from damaging the pistons or cylinders. The Fowler/Anderson bypass valve can be seen at the mid-point of the cylinder with pipes connecting it to both ends in the side elevation and the lower half of the plan. The drive for the mechanical lubricator is shown via a lever from the valve motion and a standard Midland steam brake cylinder can be seen under the cab. The tender front on both side elevation and plan is of a 3,250 gallon type and details of the intermediate buffers, drawbar and water connections are shown. The drawing is useful as it illustrates details of modifications to the front end of the tender. Sliding fire doors are illustrated.

of 3ft 9in at the buffer beam. Cast-steel motion plates of the same type as those used on the '60' Class were fitted to the rebuilt engines.

Items such as the lifeguards, draw-bars, hooks and links were re-used where possible and engines with cast-steel reversing screw brackets retained them. Cast-iron ones were replaced. The twenty Sharp, Stewart Class L engines of the '2183' Class, Nos. 403–422, were originally built with cast-iron drag boxes as opposed to fabricated ones and had them

replaced with flanged plates when they were rebuilt. The design was slightly different from the other loco-motives and so the hind ends of the frames had to be altered.

Steam brakes were fitted with the blocks ahead of the coupled wheels, the brake cylinders and pistons being recovered from the old engines where possible. Steam sanding was provided ahead of the leading coupled wheels with the sand boxes being re-used in most cases. Mechanical lubrication was employed, the Silvertown lubri-

cator being positioned on a bracket fixed to the top of the left-hand frame to the rear of the smokebox and the drive taken from the left-hand valve motion.

We believe that the 3ft 6¼in bogie wheels of the '2183', '150' and '60' Class were re-used. Others received new bogie wheels. The frames were new but some parts, such as the bot-tom plates, end stays, slides, pins, springs and brass pads, were recov-ered on at least No. 428 and above. One of the then current fashions was

11-8294 – Bogie arrangement

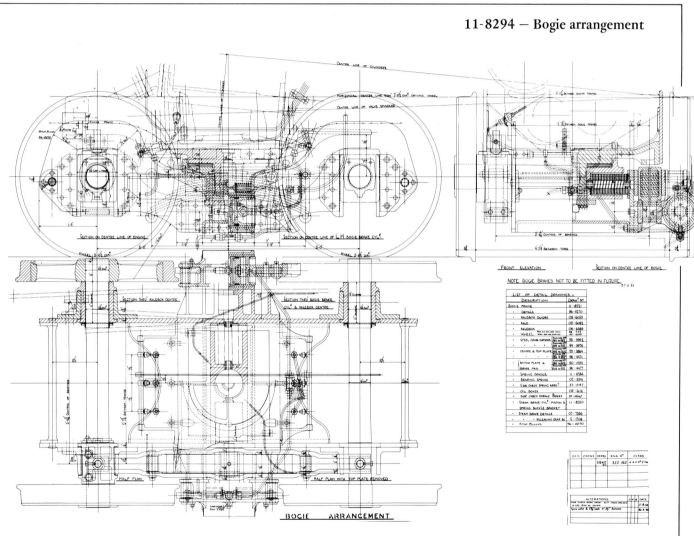

BOGIE ARRANGEMENT

Originally issued in November 1911, this drawing shows the bogie arrangement and components such as cylinders, piston valves, drain cocks and pipes that were in the immediate vicinity. It was altered in 1938 to show the later arrangement of side control, or side check, gear and again in 1940 when wider tyres were used. However, the bogie brakes, which were noted as no longer to be fitted in 1933, are still shown as it would have been deemed unnecessary to issue a new drawing and too difficult to remove all the detail from the original. As with many of the drawings issued at this time by Derby drawing office, the different sections are clearly

labelled, which makes interpretation relatively easy. Note that the locomotive frames were only cut away to clear the bogie equalising beams, not the wheels, and that only one inch sideways movement each way was allowed at the centre of the bogie. Even so, the reason for the narrowing of the locomotive frames abreast the leading bogie wheels is obvious from the drawing. As can be seen from the list of detail drawings below the front elevation, the wheels, cross girders, centre, top and bottom plates and brass pad differed slightly depending on the origin of the locomotive.

L. M. & S. R.
LOCOMOTIVE DRAWING OFFICE
DERBY

No. D11-8294

for bogie brakes and so the '483s' had them. As with other classes fitted with them, the brakes were found to be more trouble than they were worth and soon after Stanier took charge of LMS locomotive matters in 1932 they were removed. The work was carried out quite quickly as the engines passed through the shops and by November 1934 over two-thirds had been modified. To protect the leading bogie axleboxes from lubrication problems when running behind a pilot engine that was picking up water at speed, splash guards were originally fitted to the lower edges of the buffer beams, but after the Grouping they too were removed. Following trials with stronger bogie side check springs on Nos. 484, 479, 503 and two standard 2Ps, it was decided to fit them to all superheated Class 2 passenger tender engines maintained at Derby and an order to that effect was issued in December 1937. The job was done as the engines underwent general repairs. Bogie wheel suspension was via inverted leaf springs having 11 plates 5in × ⅝in.

Wheels and Axles

Locomotives already fitted with 7ft 0½in cast-steel wheels, i.e., the '2183' Class in the 403–427 series, Nos. 493–522 of the '150' Class, and '60' Class Nos. 523–562, retained them. The '1738' Class and Nos. 483–492 of the '150' Class had steel wheels fitted instead of wrought iron unless they had already been replaced. All the non-7ft engines of the '1562', '1808' and '2203' Classes with numbers below 358, between 378 and 402 or between 428 and 482 got new cast-steel wheels.

Crank axles were solid and some problems were encountered with big ends running hot. In 1935 NWO 4120 was issued to reduce the radius on the crank pin fillets, which improved matters. In 1938 an order was issued to fit built-up crank axles as the solid ones required renewal, but the first record of this happening seems to have been in 1949. We are unable to say which engines were modified except that all the survivors in 1960 had been.

The axleboxes had gunmetal facings that bore onto the backs of the wheels. They were held on by set-screws, which caused trouble by coming loose. White metal facings were used from 1939 to cure the problem, applied directly to the axleboxes in most cases but put on over the gunmetal if the axlebox and wheel wear was excessive. The coupled wheel springs were different on each axle. The leading ones were twin volute springs whilst the trailing ones were leaf springs having 15 plates, each 4½in × ½in. Hornkeeps were the type with horizontal retaining pins

We have included this picture to illustrate the cast-steel wheels as mentioned above. No. 409 was originally a member of the '2183' Class and as such entered service with 7ft 0½in diameter cast-steel driving wheels.
A. C. ROBERTS

through sockets cast into the lower extremities.

New fluted coupling rods of the Compound and '990' type, having a slightly deeper section in the middle than at the ends (sometimes called 'fishbellied'), were produced for all except the '60' Class engines. These locomotives retained their rods, which were either plain or fluted depending on whether they had been replaced when H boilers were fitted between 1906 and 1908. Nos. 533, 535 and 545 were examples of locomotives having flat-sided rods when rebuilt as '483s'. Starting in September 1920, however, the flat rods were replaced by fluted ones. As far as we are aware, only a few ever got replacement rods of any other type. Six that we know of, from photographic evidence only, that were later fitted with Stanier type plain, rectangular section rods were: Nos. 517 and 526, which got theirs sometime before 1938; No. 413, which had fluted rods until at least 1941 but later received the Stanier type; and Nos. 40453, 40541 and 40547 that had plain rods sometime after 1948.

Platform and Cab
The 8ft wide platforms were new and were raised above the coupling rods. They had continuous 5in deep angles, or 'outside frames' in Midland parlance, and footsteps ahead of the leading coupled wheels as well as at the rear. Footstep supports were riveted to the inside faces of the angles. Angled stays ran from the backs of the supports to the frames. When exhaust steam injectors were fitted, the stays were removed from the left-hand leading supports and shorter ones connecting them to the injector steam pipes were substituted. In the 1930s the corners of the steps were turned up to provide better footing when climbing on or off the engines.

Leading splashers were flush-riveted on the sides but snap-headed rivets were used on the tops. After the Grouping, snap-headed rivets were used during repairs to the beading and angles on the sides and it gradually became more common to see engines with them. Trailing splashers were contiguous with the cab and the same comments about rivets apply.

Although we illustrate all of this locomotive at page 49, we have included a close-up of the cab and crew. The fireman looks rather young whilst his driver had adopted a posed stance, with his right hand holding the regulator. Of particular interest is the arrangement of the coal rails and the live steam injector water feed handle and slaking pipe close to where the fireman was seated.

J. H. MOSS

The cab was quite spacious with four front windows, the upper two of which could be opened. The extended roof with lifting ventilator provided at least some protection from the elements for the fireman and a measure of cooling in summer. Inside there were well laid out controls and a large locker with a wooden top that provided a good seat on the fireman's side. Carriage warming was fitted to all the locomotives to the tender end only.

The first few engines rebuilt had almost completely flush-riveted cab sides but then snap-headed rivets appeared around the cut-outs, on the butt strips, or upper beading, and all around the front edges. In October 1936 instructions were issued to weld rain gutters onto the sides immediately above the cut-outs as engines went into the shops for repair. This seems to have been done fairly quickly but not to all engines. Ash and dirt found their way into the cab from all directions, but a particular annoyance to crews was the gap around the steam brake discharge

pipe. Rectification in the form of a flange brazed onto the pipe was finally ordered in 1950 but some engines never got it before withdrawal. Other modifications in the cab area included the fitting of light shields for sliding fire doors that commenced in the late 1930s but about which we have no other details.

In 1927 an order was issued to equip the tenders of seven engines with Whitaker tablet exchanging apparatus on the left-hand side. They were Nos. 404, 410, 417, 541, 542, 544 and 545.

Tender
The majority of the engines were originally coupled to 3,250 gallon Johnson tenders. Nos. 523–562, however, had 3,500 gallon examples. Known locomotive and tender pairings from about the beginning of 1928 are listed at Appendix D.

The 3,250 gallon tender construction, details and subsequent modifications were as described in *Midland Engines No. 2* for the Class 3 Belpaire goods engines and we don't propose

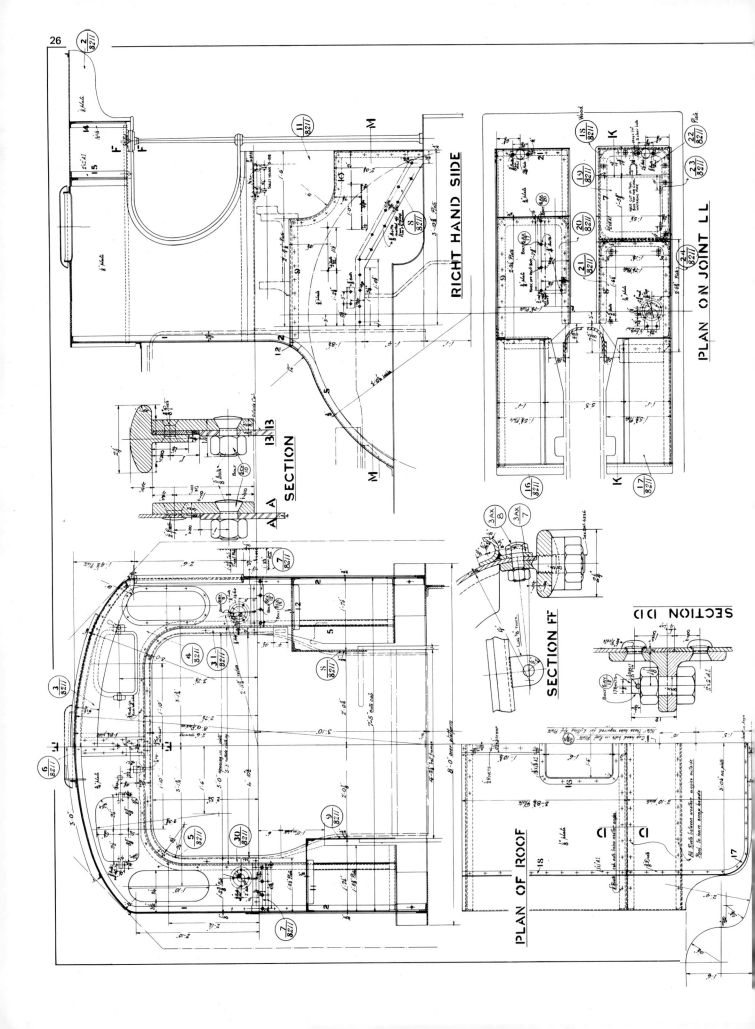

RIGHT HAND SIDE

PLAN ON JOINT LL

SECTION AA

SECTION FF

SECTION DD

PLAN OF ROOF

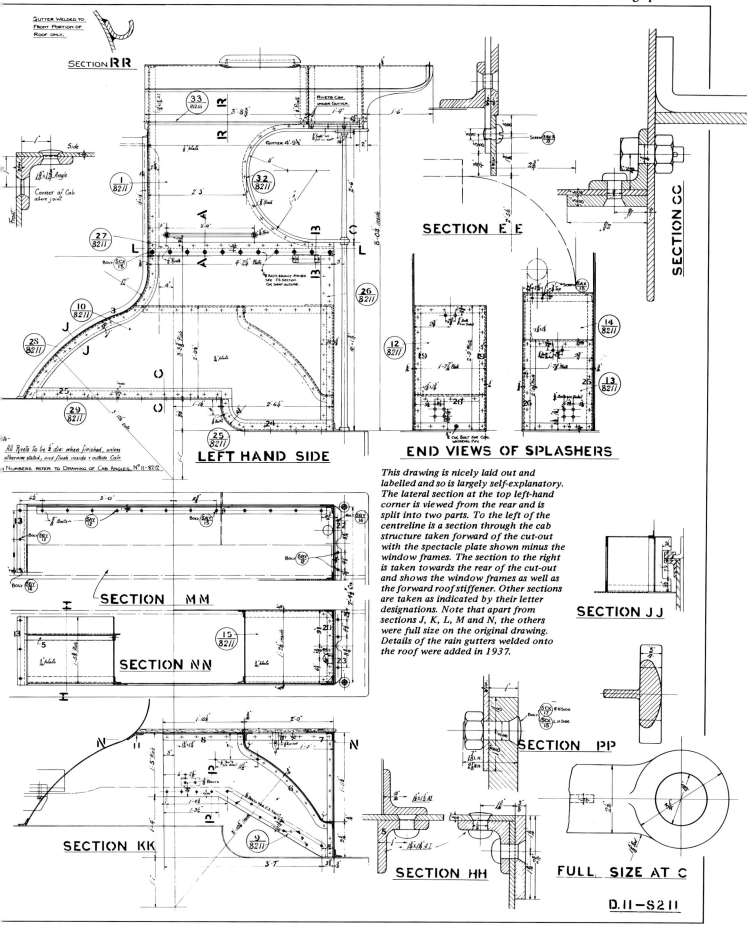

SECTION RR

GUTTER WELDED TO FRONT PORTION OF ROOF ONLY.

SECTION E E

SECTION C C

Side
Corner of Cab above joint.

END VIEWS OF SPLASHERS

LEFT HAND SIDE

Note:
All Rivets to be ⅝ dia: when finished, unless otherwise stated, and flush inside & outside Cab.
Numbers refer to Drawing of Cab Angles, No 11-8212

SECTION MM

SECTION NN

SECTION JJ

This drawing is nicely laid out and labelled and so is largely self-explanatory. The lateral section at the top left-hand corner is viewed from the rear and is split into two parts. To the left of the centreline is a section through the cab structure taken forward of the cut-out with the spectacle plate shown minus the window frames. The section to the right is taken towards the rear of the cut-out and shows the window frames as well as the forward roof stiffener. Other sections are taken as indicated by their letter designations. Note that apart from sections J, K, L, M and N, the others were full size on the original drawing. Details of the rain gutters welded onto the roof were added in 1937.

SECTION PP

SECTION KK

SECTION HH

FULL SIZE AT C

D.11-S211

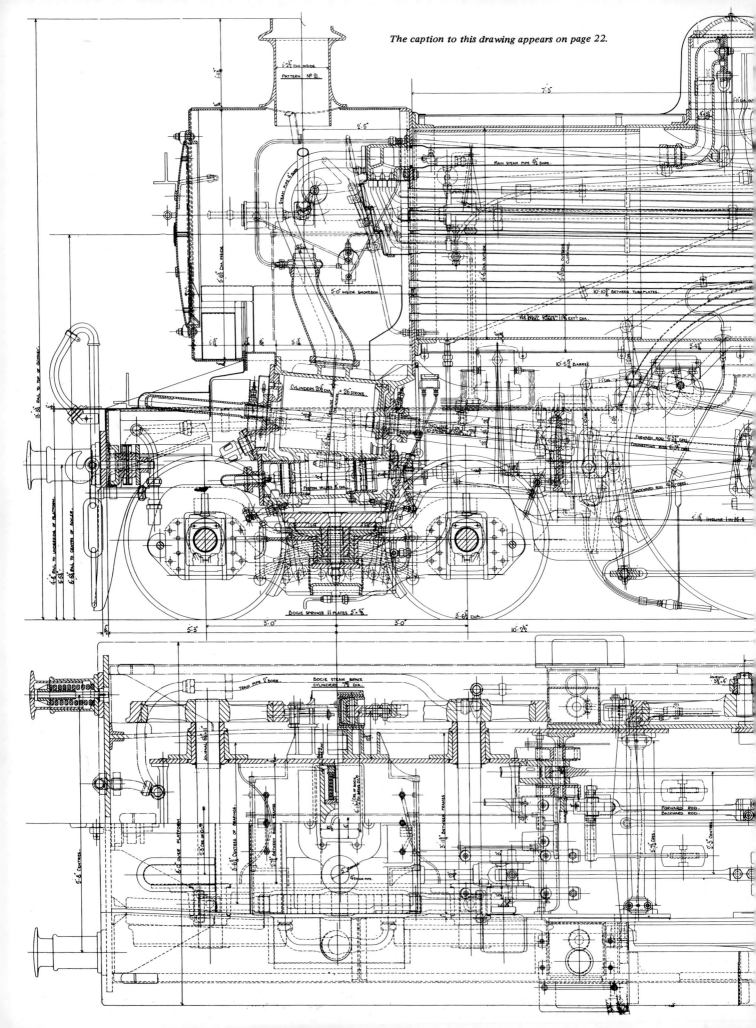

The caption to this drawing appears on page 22.

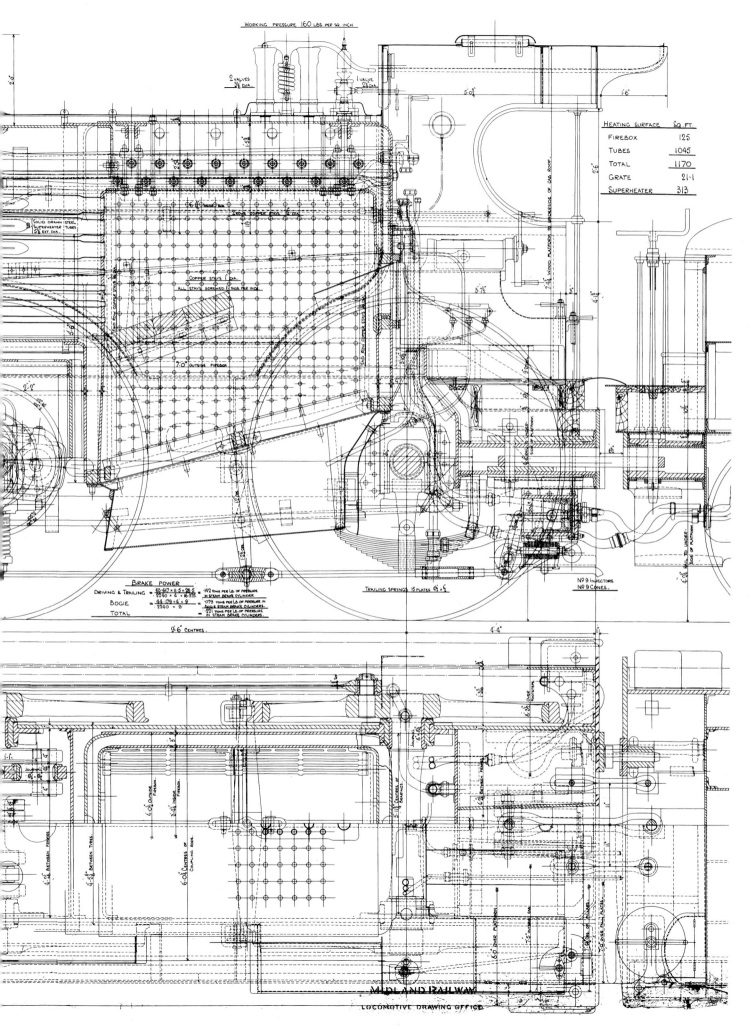

WORKING PRESSURE 160 LBS. PER SQ. INCH

2 VALVES
3⅛ DIA.

1 VALVE
2⅝ DIA

HEATING SURFACE	SQ. FT.
FIREBOX	125
TUBES	1045
TOTAL	1170
GRATE	21·1
SUPERHEATER	313

SOLID DRAWN STEEL
SUPERHEATER TUBES
5⅛ EXT. DIA.

COPPER STAYS 1¼ DIA.

COPPER STAYS 1 DIA.
ALL STAYS SCREWED 11 THDS. PER INCH.

7·0" OUTSIDE FIREBOX

BRAKE POWER

DRIVING & TRAILING = $\frac{63\cdot617 \times 11\cdot5 \times 28\cdot5}{2240 \times 4 \times 16\cdot375}$ = ·192 TONS PER LB. OF PRESSURE IN STEAM BRAKE CYLINDER.

BOGIE = $\frac{44\cdot179 \times 4 \times 9}{2240 \times 9}$ = ·079 TONS PER LB. OF PRESSURE IN BOGIE STEAM BRAKE CYLINDERS.

TOTAL = ·221 TONS PER LB. OF PRESSURE IN STEAM BRAKE CYLINDERS.

TRAILING SPRINGS 15 PLATES 4½ × ½

Nº 9 INJECTORS
Nº 9 CONES.

9·6" CENTRES.

4·4"

MIDLAND RAILWAY

LOCOMOTIVE DRAWING OFFICE

11-8216 – Driving splasher

On the left of this 1911 drawing are side views and a plan of the left-hand driving splasher. The lower of the two side elevations shows the outside face whilst above it is the inside. The scrap view at the top has details of the pad on to which the oil box was fitted. At the top right, to the left of the centreline, is a section through splasher, frame and platform and a front view to the right has some internal details shown dotted. In the lower right-hand quarter of the original drawing is a section of the splasher taken through a plane on the vertical centreline of the axle. The drawing was also used for the LMS 2Ps and the outlines of both 7ft 0½in and 6ft 9in driving wheels are shown chain dotted.

PLAIN NUMBERS REFER TO DRAWING OF
CAB ANGLES, N° 11-8212

SECTION A A

Flanging Block
same as Compound

LEFT HAND SIDE

11-8216

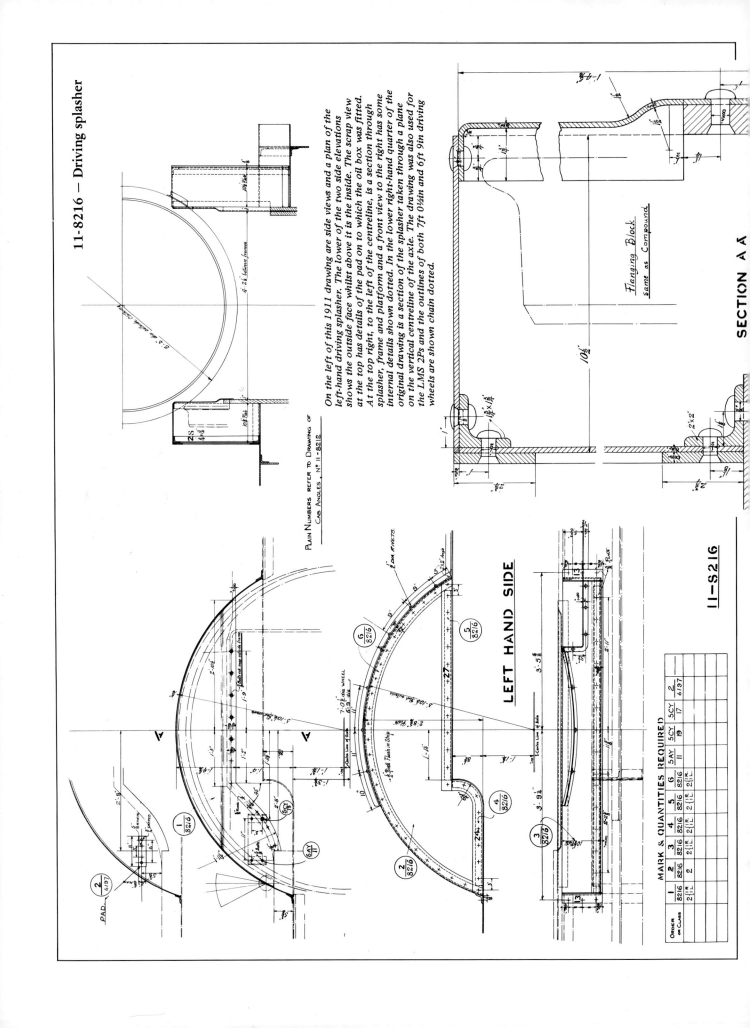

MARK & QUANTITIES REQUIRED

ORDER OR CLASS	1 8216	2 8216	3 8216	4 8216	5 8216	6 8216	5AY 11	5AY 11	5CY 19	5CY 17	2 6/97
	2{1R 1L	2	2{1R 1L	2{1R 1L	2{1R 1L	2{1R 1L					

to repeat the information here. The only difference from what we wrote in that volume, apart from one slight modification described below, is that we believe all the '483' tenders to have had water pick-up apparatus and, therefore, tank vents. Thus there were four varieties of 3,250 gallon tender that we have categorised as follows:

A 3,500 gallon tender coupled to No. 551. Compared with 3,250 gallon ones, the top edge of the upper beading on some 3,500 gallon tenders was higher and almost in line with the lower edge of the cabside butt strip, as the photograph shows.
COLLECTION
R. J. ESSERY

1. Short sides with coal rails curved at front and back, separate toolboxes, floor-mounted lockers and wooden front platforms, pillar handrails, exposed hand brake and water scoop handle spindles, and frame-mounted footsteps. Some had extension plates to the sides with sloping tops that reached forward almost to the pillar handrails and about half way up them. Some had one toolbox, others had two. If a single toolbox was fitted it was usually, but not invariably, mounted laterally on top of the bulkhead. Tenders with two boxes generally had one mounted laterally on the left-hand side and one longitudinally on the right.
2. Short sides with built-in toolboxes, coal rails ending at extended front coal plates, fire-iron supports, pillar handrails, exposed hand brake and water pick-up spindles and with or without side plates. The tenders in this category also had frame-mounted footsteps.
3. As 2 above but with separate footstep supports outside the frames.
4. Extended sides with coal rails curved front and back, built-in toolboxes, extended coal plates and fire-iron supports, commode-style handrails, steel front platforms, cast-iron hand brake and water scoop columns and separate footstep supports.

This picture of tender No. 419 illustrates the front of a 3,250 and should be compared with the similar but larger 3,500 gallon tender above.   AUTHORS' COLLECTION

The 3,500 gallon tenders were almost indistinguishable from unmodified 3,250 gallon ones. There were two types attached to '483s'. The ones coupled to engines 543–562, had 4ft 2in deep tanks so that the top of the beading was virtually in line with the lower edge of the butt strip on the locomotive cab side, whereas on 3,250 gallon ones with 3ft 11in deep tanks it was appreciably lower. This is shown in some of the photographs we have reproduced. Engines 523–542, however, had 3,500 gallon tenders with 'side pockets' at the front of the coal space and tank sides only 4ft 0in deep. The only modifications to any 3,500 gallon tenders originally attached to a '483' were, as far as we know, the short side extensions and, on at least one, built-in toolboxes.

In Midland days there was another variation seen on a few tenders that had been originally to do with the fitting of tender cabs. Rather than the short extensions to the side plates described above, they had full-depth rectangular extensions. These were attached with snap-head rivets, reaching from the side plates almost to the pillars and from the lower edges of the upper beading to the platform. Locomotives we know to have been coupled to such tenders before the Grouping were 500 and 535.

Following later changes there were other types of 3,500 gallon tenders paired with some '483s'. In June 1929 No. 520 got a straight-sided 7ft 0in + 6ft 9in wheelbase Deeley one that

was originally built for a '990' Class 4–4–0. It was one of the narrow platform Deeley tenders on which the platform only projected beyond the tank sides for a short distance at the front and rear. Others came from '700' Class 4–4–0s and were attached to Nos. 455, 488, 548, 553, 555 and 557, recorded in the history cards as 'at' December 1931. This means that the actual date when the engines received those tenders was possibly some time before that. For all except 548 and 555 they were similar to those coupled to the rest of the '483s' but with higher platforms and deeper platform angles having fillets to the buffer beam and contiguous footstep supports. The built-in toolboxes were also different and were the full-width

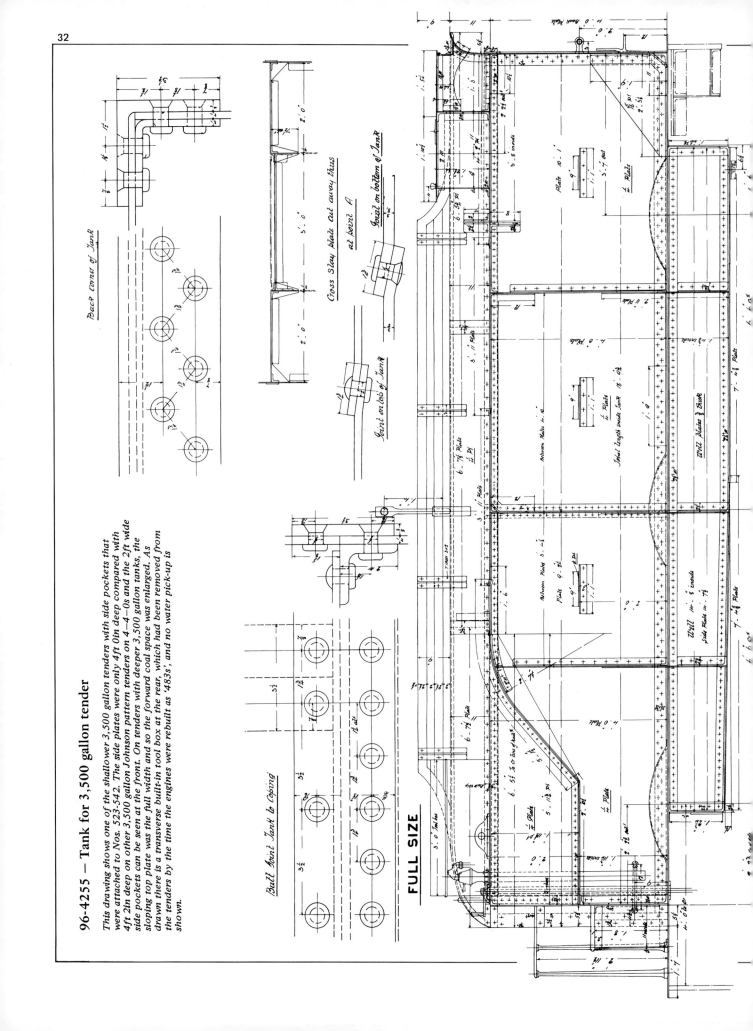

96-4255 – Tank for 3,500 gallon tender

This drawing shows one of the shallower 3,500 gallon tenders with side pockets that were attached to Nos. 523-542. The side plates were only 4ft 0in deep compared with 4ft 2in deep on other 3,500 gallon Johnson pattern tenders on 4–4–0s and the 2ft wide side pockets can be seen at the front. On tenders with deeper 3,500 gallon tanks, the sloping top plate was the full width and so the forward coal space was enlarged. As drawn there is a transverse built-in tool box at the rear, which had been removed from the tenders by the time the engines were rebuilt as '483s', and no water pick-up is shown.

FULL SIZE

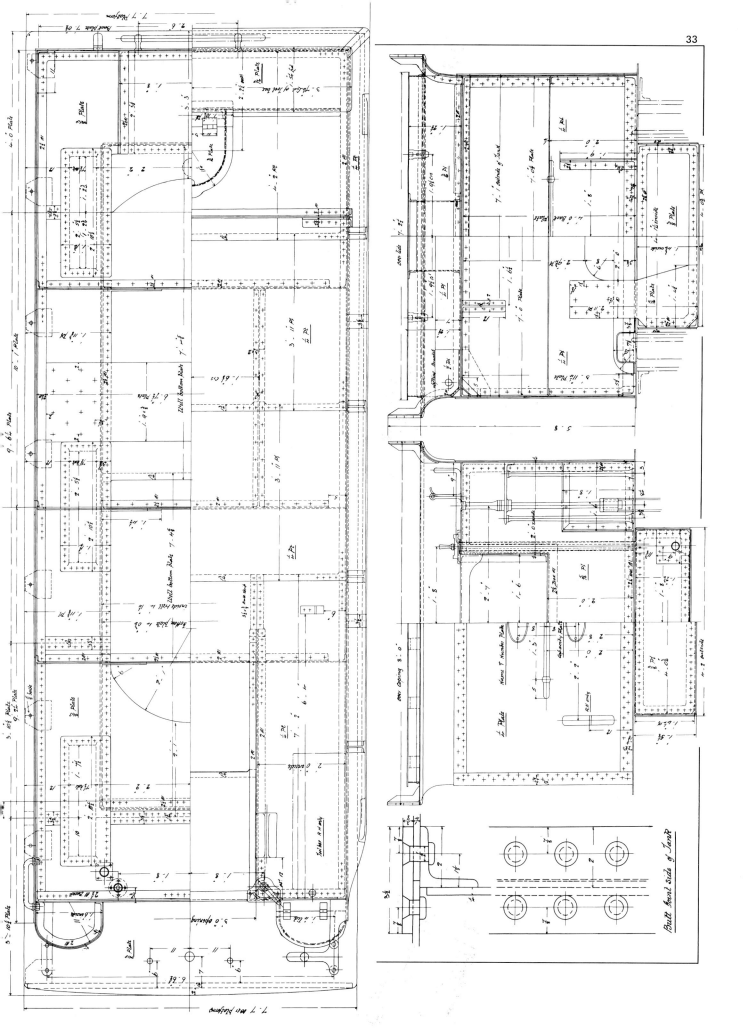

96-4327 – Frame for tender

In Midland Engines No. 2 we reproduced a general arrangement drawing of a 3,250 gallon Johnson tender, albeit with early toolbox and coupling and without water pick-up apparatus. We have been unable to find any later arrangement drawings of the type and so, for details of a 3,250 gallon tender, refer readers to that volume with the provisos above. Although this drawing, first issued in 1896, is annotated as showing the frame arrangement for 3,250 gallon tenders, it is referred to in drawing lists as applying to 3,500 gallon ones as well. The frame design for 13ft wheelbase tenders was virtually the same with only a few minor variations up to 1908. Along the top of the drawing is the left-hand inside frame, which was made from 5/8in plate, with the one-inch thick outside frame below it. Under that are side elevation and plan of the frame arrangement. The plan is split in two. Above the centreline is a view from above the frames whilst below it is a section taken on varying planes. Down the left-hand side are sections through the front dragbox and an end view of the front buffer beam. At the top right are a later section through the inside and outside frames (A-A), a longitudinal section through the rear dragbox (C-C) and a lateral half-section through the rear dragbox (D-D). There is also a lateral half section and half rear view of the front dragbox. To the right of the plan is a vertical section through the rear dragbox, above the centreline, and a rear view of the buffer beam below it. The other sections were full size on the original drawing and show rivet and angle details at various points. Section D shows the ¼in leather tank. Note the horizontal tie-bars between the brackets on the sides of the frames and the spacers that were placed between the lower edges of the outside frames between the wheels. The rear one was moved if a tender was fitted with water pick-up apparatus.

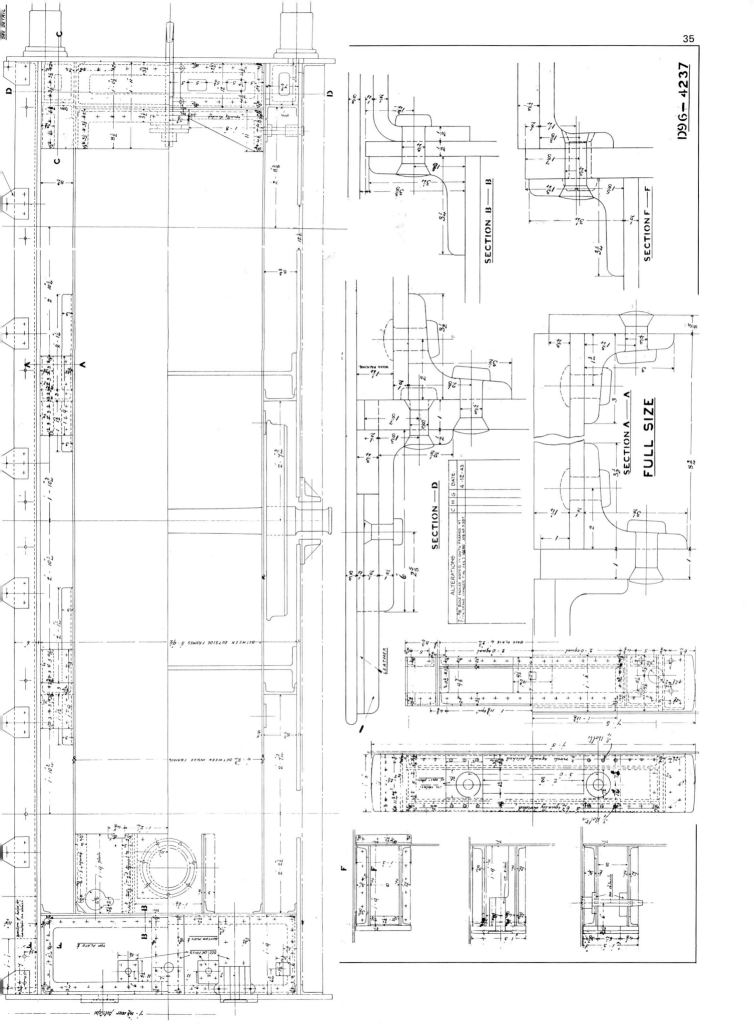

One type of replacement tender attached to a '483' is shown here with No. 548. Originally a 4,500 gallon bogie 'water cart', it was rebuilt as a 6-wheeler and coupled to a '700' Class 4–4–0. During its lifetime No. 548 had two such tenders, the first sometime before December 1931 and another a year later, which are described in the text. The locomotive still had bogie brakes, bypass valves and Ramsbottom safety valves with an oval base cover when the photograph was taken.   D. IBBOTSON

One of the engines that acquired a tender of a different type was No. 555. It was photographed in August 1937 at Derby Works with its 3,500 gallon one from a withdrawn '700' Class 4–4–0. Unlike the other 'Belpaire' tenders coupled to '483s', it had no vertical centre beading. Note that the platform was higher than the usual tenders paired with these locomotives and that it lined up with the locomotive platform. The upper footsteps were also in line. The deep platform angle and fillet at the buffer beam can be seen, as can the footstep support riveted to the back of the angle. The built-in toolboxes were different from those on other '483' 3,500 gallon tenders, being full width with concave corners (these toolboxes are described in Midland Engines No. 2*).*

type with concave corners, described in *Midland Engines No. 2* as fitted to 3,500 gallon tenders coupled to Class 3 Belpaire 0–6–0s numbered below 3815. No. 555's was the same but without the vertical butt strips on the tank sides. Some of these tenders were later replaced – see Appendix D for details. No. 548 had two replacement tenders that were Deeley rebuilds of 4,500 gallon bogie tenders and were originally coupled to Class 3 engines Nos. 732 and 733. They had the longer 13ft 9in wheelbase, straight sides and narrow platforms that only extended beyond the sides for a short distance at front and rear. They differed from the '990' Class tender in that behind the platform angles the sides could be seen turned under to meet the frames. Separate footstep supports were attached to the insides of the angles at front and rear. Although the toolbox fascia had the same concave cornered shape as the toolboxes on the 3,500 gallon Belpaire tenders, the toolboxes themselves were only as wide as the horizontal top plate and had vertical sides. No. 548's history card records the first of these tenders as being coupled to it by December 1931 and the second a year later. In 1949, however, it reverted to a 3,250 gallon tender. Another rebuilt bogie tender,

Photographed at Coventry c.1950, this picture of the tender rear of No. 40405 brought back memories for one of us. Coal spillage on the rear of the tender was not unusual, good firemen threw it forward into the coal space, others left it there. This type of tender was not ideal from the standpoint of storage, so most firemen placed fire-irons at the rear of the tender, as seen here.
                                                                    H. F. WHEELLER

this time an ex-4,100 gallon one originally attached to 4—4—0 No. 737, was coupled to No. 40542 in 1955.

Several engines were paired with straight-sided LMS standard 3,500 gallon tenders. No. 489 was seen at Leeds with one *circa* 1939 but we have no other information and the change is not recorded on the engine's history card. In the mid to late 1950s Nos. 40407, 40416, 40453, 40487, 40504 and 40540 had ones with small frame slots, beading, flush rivets and no coal rails, whereas those attached to Nos. 40421, 40511, 40537 and 40559 were rebuilt with 3,500 gallon tanks on Johnson 2,950 gallon frames and differed by having large frame slots. Coal rails were fitted to the ones behind 40537 and 40559, the latter being later transferred to No. 40489. In 1957 No. 40491 got a snap-riveted LMS standard 3,500 gallon tender that still had gangway doors, even though the locomotive wasn't equipped for them.

In the early 1950s Nos. 40402, 40413, 40461, 40536 and 40553 received 3,500 gallon tenders with flared sides that had originally been built for Class 4 goods engines. They were similar to earlier 3,500 gallon tenders but with smaller slots in the frames, without holes ahead of the leading axleboxes, and with the footsteps mounted on separate plates. No. 40402 was coupled to an early type with short sides, pillar handrails, beading around the tank sides (but no central butt strip), coal rails that finished at the front plate, and countersunk rivets. The others had full-length sides, commode-style handrails, coal rails curved at front and rear, and snap-headed rivets. Both types had built-in toolboxes that had vertical sides and were not the full width of the tender.

With the above information and the known pairings listed in Appendix D, we hope to have given a reasonable account of the '483s' tender history but, being realistic, there may well be points that we have missed. If you have additional information we would be only too pleased to hear of it.

A category 2, 3,250 gallon tender with short extensions to the side plates is shown to advantage in this picture of No. 511 piloting a Bristol express at Birmingham New Street. This picture shows the elliptical water capacity plate immediately below the top lamp iron on the tank whilst above it, just below the beading, we can see the rectangular LMS number plate, in this case bearing No. 2053. As noted in the text, some engines did not have exhaust steam injectors fitted, 511 being one of them. The livery was wartime black with gilt or yellow transfers shaded vermilion and the general air of filth and neglect was in stark contrast to the condition of even the worst engines in Midland days. COLLECTION R. J. ESSERY

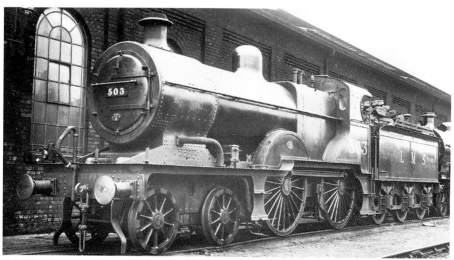

Modifications were not applied consistently. Although No. 503 had its bogie brakes and bypass valves removed, the corners of its footsteps turned up and an exhaust steam injector fitted before being photographed at Leicester in 1936, it still had Ramsbottom safety valves with a circular base cover. As discussed in the text, some engines appear to have been plain black at this time and we can find no trace of lining on this one despite long and close scrutiny. The letters and numbers also appear unshaded. One of the 1914 rebuilds, the engine had acquired a fair number of snap-head rivets but was still without extra washout holes. Its tender was one of the 3,500 gallon type with a 4ft 2in high tank. REAL PHOTOGRAPHS

This picture of engine No. 409 illustrates an example of a Category 4 tender as described on page 31 with the commode handles clearly visible. COLLECTION R. J. ESSERY

This delightful view of No. 447 at Buxton, taken on 3rd May 1934, illustrates a Class 2P at the head of an ordinary stopping passenger train. As they were displaced from more important work by larger more modern locomotives, the Class 2P found regular employment upon such work. H. C. CASSERLEY

THE ENGINES IN SERVICE

One of the commonly aired perceptions about the '483s' is that they were long-lived and economical engines because they were only used on light duties. This is often attributed to poor valves and strangled steam passages resulting in performances that didn't allow them to be worked too hard. Whilst it is true that their boiler pressure was low for the cylinder size, the front end design left something to be desired in terms of valve events and the steam circuit was fairly tortuous, in Midland and pre-war LMS days they were

employed on many express duties and were far from lightly loaded for their size. The LMS loading book shows that the full load for a Class 2 engine was generally half that of a 'Royal Scot' and about two-thirds that of a Horwich mogul. For example, between Liverpool and Manchester the figures were 225 tons for a '483' compared with 345 tons for a mogul and 450 tons for a Class 6 engine. Limited and Special Limit loads were in the same proportion, with a '483' taking 200 and 180 tons respectively. Even on the bank from

Manchester Victoria to Miles Platting they could be called on to take 155 tons unaided. Later on they were mainly used on secondary passenger and some freight duties and after nationalisation were often seen on such tasks as station pilots. They were notably economical as regards maintenance and repair costs; in fact, they were the most cost-effective of any LMS engines in a study undertaken in 1926 and became the yardstick by which other locomotives were judged.[13] Despite their shortcomings, they were worthwhile and

No. 459 is seen here at Ais Gill with a stopping freight train in 1929. Although originally employed on express passenger work, in later years they were to be found on stopping freight trains and even Sunday ballast trains, as one of us recalls. Not the most suitable engine for such work.
L & GRP

We believe this picture, taken in August 1929, was at Worcester and shows Nottingham's No. 409 probably shortly after it had arrived with a stopping passenger train. Note the driver, who was either oiling or examining the inside motion.
J. A. G. H. COLTAS

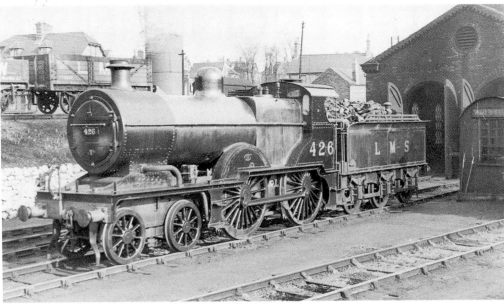

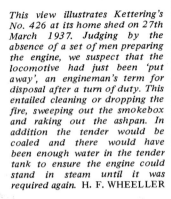

This view illustrates Kettering's No. 426 at its home shed on 27th March 1937. Judging by the absence of a set of men preparing the engine, we suspect that the locomotive had just been 'put away', an engineman's term for disposal after a turn of duty. This entailed cleaning or dropping the fire, sweeping out the smokebox and raking out the ashpan. In addition the tender would be coaled and there would have been enough water in the tender tank to ensure the engine could stand in steam until it was required again. **H. F. WHEELLER**

useful engines with which a fair proportion of bread-and-butter revenue was earned. Some commentators, such as E.S. Cox, have decried both their worth and their being used as the basis for an LMS standard design. Whilst acknowledging the expertise of some of these gentlemen, the facts of the 1926 study remain and we can't help but think that the highly unpopular 'Midlandisation' of the LMS in its early years may have attracted to the locomotives more than their fair share of adverse comment. The points we made earlier about the possible reasons for their rebuilding in the first place and the economics of running a railway in 1912 should also be borne in mind. That they lasted until 1962 surely indicates that they were worth their keep.

Preparation and disposal were relatively straightforward and the layout of cab and controls was generally appreciated by enginemen. The G7S boiler was a good steam generator and, although not as well matched to the cylinders as it was on the LMS-built 2Ps, gave firemen little cause for concern when on the road. The tenders' main drawbacks were that they didn't have any doors in the front plates and the vents were inside the coal space (these comments are made about the original tenders). The first meant that firemen either had to climb over the front plate, or bulkhead as it was often known, when bringing coal forward or to try and

dislodge the coal using the long rake and bring it down the sloping tank top. With low-fronted tenders the first option was possible but on modified ones with raised coal plates it was easy to get above the loading gauge in the process, with obvious potential results. The vents were prone to picking up dust and small pieces of coal that could then find their way into the tank, especially if the tender was piled high as was often the case. Unlike some other tenders that suffered from the same problem, they had no rear bulkhead behind which the vents could be re-sited.

There were a few trials of such things as heat-resistant paints and different types of white-metalling on some of the engines. None was particularly significant, however, and we don't propose to enumerate them here. One locomotive, No. 558, was noted in its history card as receiving the Tilbury section Hudd ATC apparatus in June 1934. The equipment was recorded as having come from No. 562, although there is no record of that engine having it. We have no further details and have not seen any photographs showing the apparatus fitted to either engine, both of which were shedded at Kentish Town at the time.

They were quite strongly built machines and, once the unnecessary complications of bogie brakes and bypass valves had been removed, were reliable and fairly straight-

forward to maintain. The axleboxes could have been more generous but their record of hot boxes does not seem to have been as bad as some of their contemporaries. It has been stated many times in the past that this was because they were used on fairly light duties for most of their lives. In our view, however, this is simply not true and at least up to the mid-1930s they were called on to work as hard as any other Class 2 engines. There were some problems with connecting rod big end wear and overheating, which seem to have been cured by the alterations to the crankpin fillets described earlier. All in all, and despite their shortcomings and detractors, we think that they were perfectly adequate engines for their intended tasks and gave sterling service.

Oil Burning

During both the 1921 miners' strike and the general strike of 1926, some of the class were converted to oil burning. We know of two methods of fitting the fuel tanks onto the tender in 1921. One, which only seems to have been used on No. 527, involved six small tanks being stacked and secured together by end plates and strapping, the whole ensemble then being fixed into the coal space. There were four tanks in the bottom row and two above them. The more common arrangement was for two larger tanks with distance pieces to be fitted onto saddles in the coal space and strapped down to the coal rails. The larger tanks were 3ft 7⅛in diameter and 8ft long. In 1926 the latter method was certainly used but we have seen no evidence of the smaller tanks. From the limited information we have, however, we can't state that they definitely were not used. No. 480 was apparently seen with flat-sided oil tanks but we have no other information on it. Engines selected for alteration in 1921 included Nos. 403, 421, 490, 491, 495, 500–4, 510, 527, 540, 547, 550 and 560. Oil-filling facilities were provided at Derby, Bedford, Kentish Town, Bristol, Gloucester and Leeds and forty old tenders were modified for carrying and storing fuel oil. In 1926 we believe that Nos. 362, 364, 479, 480, 484, 487, 492, 500, 504, 506, 527, 555, and 557–9 received oil-burning apparatus.

Since the light-burning oil was simply gravity fed to the burners, the tanks were angled down towards the front to ensure a constant feed under all conditions. The main oil shutoff valve was mounted on the tender front and from it a flexible pipe led under the fall plate to a flow valve mounted under the footplate. This valve was operated by a spindle sticking up through the floorboards to a handle on the fireman's side of the cab. With it he could regulate the flow of oil to the burner. Another metal-shielded, flexible pipe led from the flow valve to a burner mounted in a plate that fitted into the lower part of the firehole and replaced the bottom door. The burner was connected not only to the oil feed, but to the steam supply normally used for carriage heating that could also be controlled by the fireman. Steam was directed into the firebox through a slot in the burner that was immediately below the oil nozzle and designed to produce a fan-shaped jet. This steam jet caught the oil as it issued from the nozzle, atomised it and sprayed it into the firebox where it was ignited. The result was an intensely hot flame that spread out through the firebox. The firebars were covered with broken firebrick that would become almost incandescent and simulated the normal fire bed. When the engine was standing, the oil could be turned off and wood,

or sometimes coal, burned on the grate to keep the firebox at least partially heated and to provide ignition when the oil was turned on again. Problems were found with differential expansion, because the front of the firebox became much hotter than the back, and the angle of the burner flame needed constant adjustment to avoid burning either the firebars or the brick arch. Enginemen were also somewhat wary of the pronounced 'whump' that accompanied ignition

of the oil, and a sticking or stiff flow valve could make it difficult for the fireman to adjust the oil feed properly. This often led to incomplete combustion, lots of black smoke and sooted tubes. The system worked reasonably well overall, however, and Roland Bond, later to become CME of British Railways, said that it was considered a worthwhile temporary measure. Later trials in 1948 showed that 69lb of oil produced the same evaporation as 100lb of coal.

Of the methods of fitting oil tanks during the 1921 miners' strike, No. 527's 3,500 gallon tender here demonstrates what was possibly the only example of the 6-small-tank version. The tanks were fixed together with end plates and strapping and placed in the coal space on the level part of the water tank top as a unit. Each one had a question-mark-shaped vent towards the rear and the water tank vents were moved back to accommodate them. The locomotive still had flush riveting on its smokebox and the coupling rod fluting was unpainted. The photograph provides a good illustration of the mismatch between engine and tender footsteps and platforms. Note the depth of the wooden platform built onto the front of the tender in order to line up with the footplate. The top edge of the upper beading on the tender seems to have been lined. Whilst not unknown, this was not as common as would be suggested by casual glances at photographs. Many instances of what looks like lining are reflections from the top edges of the beading but in this case examination of the tender rear seems to confirm that it was lined. Note that there was no tender number plate.

W. L. GOOD (554)

The more usual method of oil storage on tenders is seen on the 3,250 gallon unmodified one attached to No. 487 in 1926. Two large tanks with saddles and spacers had been used instead of the six smaller ones and were strapped to the coal rails. The vents can be seen on the splasher sides and there was definitely no lining on the top of the upper tender beading.

COLLECTION R. J. ESSERY

PAINTING AND NUMBERS

In Midland ownership the '483s' were painted in simplified crimson lake livery. This style continued, with a few alterations, into the Grouping. From 1928 lined black became their official style. During the austerity years the lining was omitted from repainted engines, then, after nationalisation, either plain black or mixed traffic lined livery was applied. Within these broad statements there were many variations and anomalies, so we will discuss each phase in turn.

Crimson Lake

By the time the '483s' were rebuilt, the process of change in painting and numbering styles that took place in the 1900s was complete and the livery for passenger engines had settled down to a period of relative stability and commonality between classes. The paint scheme for the whole of the engines' time in Midland ownership was as outlined in the adjacent panel.[14]

The height of the tender side numerals was 18in not including the shading. Black edging below the platform was specified as ¾–1in thick whilst above it was 2–2½in. This does not seem to have been followed around the cab cut-outs, however, which appear to have had only about an inch of black around the beading. Perhaps it was the beading that caused the variation. Flat beading had no specified line thickness, it was just painted black with the pale straw on the edge. Pale straw lining was specified as ⅜in thick below the platform and ⅛in above it. Tender side, smokebox door and power classification figures were all scroll and serif.

Although this scheme was fairly consistent, there was some variance as shown *(right)*. Additionally, some tenders appear to have had pale straw lining on the top edges of the upper beading. Many photographs that seem to indicate this are misleading as close inspection shows the 'lining' to be light reflecting from the edge of the beading. There are sufficient cases that are unmistakeably lining, however, to prove that the

In the 1920s at least two engines had serif buffer beam lettering. One of them was No. 509, which is seen double-heading an up express near King's Norton in July 1921 with 2–4–0 No. 126. The coupling rod fluting appears to have been unpainted, although it is difficult to be sure, whilst the smokebox door ring and hinges were polished steel. W. L. GOOD (632)

Boiler and firebox clothing	Crimson lake. Front clothing band black, fine lined pale straw on rear edge. Other clothing bands crimson lake. Angle iron next to cab black, fine lined pale straw on front edge of vertical and horizontal portions and around the shoulders only – not on curved portion around cab splasher tops Dome cover, safety valves and base cover crimson lake. Occasionally the tops of the Ramsbottom valves were polished brass. Whistle polished brass. Ejector crimson lake with polished brass & copper pipework and details. Handrails crimson lake and black to match adjacent colour.
Smokebox	Black. Handrail black. Number plate black with raised characters polished iron. District number plate black with characters and border polished iron. Chimney black. Superheater damper control gear, where fitted, black, sometimes with valve casing bare metal. 'Dog ring', or smokebox door seat, and hinges polished steel.
Platform	Black. Platform angle crimson lake edged black, fine lined pale straw on lower and vertical edges only. Footstep supports crimson lake edged black, fine lined pale straw on inside but not around upper footsteps or along top edge. Footsteps black. Grab handles black but sometimes bare metal – possibly due to wear. Front plate above buffer beam crimson lake. Drag beam black. Mechanical lubricator black.
Splashers	Sides crimson lake. Beading black, fine lined pale straw adjacent to inner edge. Tops and angle iron between splashers and boiler clothing black.
Buffer plank	Vermilion edged black, fine lined pale straw on inside, generally with gilt, shaded blue and black sans serif 'MR' either side of coupling hook, just inside frame rivets (but see below). Buffer housings vermilion, casting beads black, fine lined pale straw to rear. Buffers, couplings and coupling hook bare metal. Vacuum standpipe appears to have matched adjacent colour, i.e., black above platform, crimson lake between platform and buffer beam and vermilion next to beam. Lower end black, fine lined pale straw adjacent to buffer beam lower lining but no lining above that. Bogie splash guards black.
Frames	Inside faces vermilion. Outside faces black behind front sand boxes. Ahead of front sand boxes crimson lake edged black, fine lined pale straw on inside of lower edge only. Life guards, brake gear, sanding gear, footstep support stays and bypass valves black. Builder's plates crimson lake with polished brass raised characters and border.

Apart from the late-Midland livery changes already noted and the repositioning of the Derby makers' plates, the only difference in painting and numbering from pre-Grouping days in this view of No. 450 at Derby in October 1923 was the absence of buffer beam lettering and cabside crests. The engine was one of the last to be rebuilt and was not completed until 1923. The light reflections clearly show the number of snap-head and pan-head rivets used on the frames, platform angle and footstep supports. There was no lock-up valve on the firebox and the casing for the Ramsbottom valve bases was circular. The tender was one of the 'fully modified' 3,250 gallon ones with built-in toolboxes, steel front platform and cast-iron brake and water scoop columns. The side sheets were extended with commode style hand rails fitted to them and there were separate footstep supports. The coupling rod fluting was black and although at first glance the top of the upper tender beading appears to have been lined, this is, in fact, light reflection.

W. L. GOOD (1294)

practice was not unknown, albeit not very common.

There were some livery changes after the First World War. Around 1921 at least two engines, Nos. 509 and 514, had serif buffer beam lettering but whether this was an anomaly or the start of a trend we are unable to say. At around the same time, possibly slightly later but certainly before the Grouping, three other things began to change. A start was made on moving the Derby makers' plates from the front frames above the platform to the sides of the splashers but not many engines appear to have been altered prior to 1923.[15] Also, the previously polished steel smokebox door ring and hinges were painted black and, perversely, the black paint was omitted from coupling rod fluting. There were also at least three engines, Nos. 504, 506 and 507, that had polished steel hinges and handrails on their smokebox doors but painted dog rings in 1921. Whether this was an intermediate stage in the process of making the whole 'front end' black and whether any more locomotives were so treated, we don't know. It is quite possible that the cleaning practice at individual sheds would also have determined such details to some extent.

At first the only change after the Grouping was for repainted engines to have the lettering omitted from the front buffer beams and the

Wheels and axles	Wheels black with fine pale straw line around face of tyre adjacent to its inner edge. Tyres black. Axles vermilion, ends black. Side rods bare metal with black fluting.
Motion	Weight shaft, bearings, motion plate, weights, valve spindle guides and lifting links vermilion. Reversing rod crimson lake with forked end and link bare metal. Rest of motion bare metal. Oil cups brass.
Bogie	Insides of frames and stretchers vermilion. Outsides of frames and brakes black. Wheels and axles as before.
Cab	Front crimson lake above boiler handrail level, black below. Opening window frames polished brass. Sides crimson lake. Beading around lower sides and cut-outs black, fine lined pale straw adjacent to inner edge. On cut-outs the black was carried about one inch onto the sides. The waist level beading, or butt strip, was lined pale straw adjacent to the bottom edge but there was no black edging or lining at the front edge of the upper cab side or along the rain strip. Pillar handrails black or polished metal. Grab handles crimson lake but occasionally appear to have been bare metal. Company crest transfer in lower panel – for positioning see photographs. Power class 2 in small brass numerals on upper sides in front of cut-outs. Roof crimson lake up to rainstrips. Between rainstrips black, although some photographs and anecdotal evidence suggest that it may have been crimson lake on at least some engines. Inside cab crimson lake edged black, fine lined pale straw on inside up to waist level. Above waist level grained oak finish edged black, fine lined pale straw on inside. Firebox back plate black, roof white (rapidly becoming cream).
Tender frames, platform, buffer beam & wheels	Inside faces of frames black. Outsides crimson lake edged black, fine lined pale straw on inside on lower edges, vertical edges and around cut-outs, lower footsteps and brake shaft bearings but not around upper footsteps. Often the pale straw was not carried around the brake shaft bearings. Footsteps, springs, pillars, buckles, axleboxes and guides black, Platform black. Buffer beam, buffers, casings, couplings and vacuum pipe as locomotive but no lettering on beam and no crimson strip above it. Carriage warming pipe black. Wheels as locomotive.
Tender tank	Top black. Tank vents black. Sides and rear crimson lake. Beading black, fine lined pale straw on inside except central vertical beading on sides, which was crimson lake. Top edge of upper beading on sides generally unlined but see text Flare crimson lake, top edge black, fine lined pale straw. Grab handles crimson lake, sometimes bare metal. Pillar handrails black or bare metal. Coal rails black. Running number in 18in gold transfers with black shading, positioned with two numerals to the rear of the centre vertical beading. Number and capacity plates crimson lake with polished brass characters.
Tender front	Crimson lake edged black, fine lined pale straw on inside. Opening to coal space edged black, fine lined pale straw on outside. Shovelling plate bare metal. Top of bulkhead black. Inside faces of sides forward of bulkhead appear to have been black on tenders with separate tool boxes and the toolboxes also black. Built-in tool boxes sometimes crimson lake, fine lined pale straw on front, tops black.

One of the 1914 rebuilds was No. 482. It is seen here in 1923 with the fairly rare 'L M S' in individual letters on the cab sides. The engine and unmodified 3,250 gallon tender appear to have been unaltered from their original 1914 condition. **REAL PHOTOGRAPHS**

One of the last engines rebuilt under Midland auspices in 1922, No. 400 displays the common 1923-28 LMS livery. The addition of the gilt transfer 'P' to the power class on the upper cab side, however, suggests that the picture was taken in or after 1928. The condition of the locomotive and its category 2 modified tender were typical of 1920s renewals but note that a row of washout plugs had appeared on the firebox side above the handrail. LMS ownership is indicated by the crest on the lower cab side. Either the figure '4' had been replaced on the tender or the cleaners had not reached the others. **LENS OF SUTTON**

A handful of '483s' were painted in the crimson lake passenger livery with cabside numerals and tender letters. One such was No. 536 pictured at Nottingham on an unknown date. As the photograph clearly shows, the 10in numerals were different from the Midland style and not as attractive. The tender was one of the unmodified, single toolbox variety with the box mounted longitudinally on the right-hand side. The locomotive, whilst still fitted with bogie brakes and bypass valves, had lost its lock-up safety valve whilst retaining the long casing to the valve bases and did not have any washout plugs on its firebox sides. **COLLECTION R. J. ESSERY**

Midland crest from the cab sides. No. 450 was repainted in this way, without any signs of ownership, in early 1923. In May 1923 the LMS decided that all passenger locomotives would have the company crest, and goods engines small individual gold letters 'LMS' on the cab sides. In the main that is what happened, but some passenger locomotives repainted in 1923 got the lettering before the transfer crests were available. Examples of '483s' with the letters were Nos. 332, 439, 497, 507, 520, 530 and 551. Even though the black paint in coupling rod fluting had begun to disappear in late Midland days, there were still instances of repainted engines having it after the Grouping, Nos. 419, 423, 450 and 477 being known examples. There were also instances of repainted locomotives still having the Derby makers' plates on the sides of the frames, e.g., Nos. 423 and 551, although the majority continued the practice begun by the Midland of moving them to the splashers. After a short while things settled down and the usual appearance of a '483' before 1928 was as described for the Midland livery with the following alterations:

Buffer beam devoid of lettering.
LMS makers' plates on splasher sides.
Coupling rod fluting bare metal.
Smokebox door and front all black.

LMS 'button' crest (or 'coat of arms') on lower cab sides.

In December 1927 it was decided that the locomotive running number would henceforth be carried on the cab sides in 10in imitation gold characters with black shading.[16] Company ownership would be displayed in 14in serif letters, also imitation gold with black shading, on the sides of the tenders. Only a few '483s' received this livery, the ones we know of being Nos. 407, 503, 536 and 545, which probably had the numbers hand painted as transfers were not available so soon after the change-over. The numerals were similar in style to the Midland ones but weren't quite as attractive. The letters were spaced at 40in centres with the 'M' immediately to the rear of the vertical butt strip.

Early in 1928 Midland Division tenders were given their own distinctive numbers, rather than carrying the locomotive number as was Midland practice. The numbers were displayed on rectangular brass plates with black backgrounds fixed to the tender rears.

LMS Black

On 7th February 1928 instructions were issued that henceforth only five classes were to be painted red – the 'Royal Scots', 'Claughtons', L&Y Class 8 engines, 'Prince of Wales' Class and the standard Compounds. This was cancelled on 25th February but then reinstated on 24th March. As with the Midland trend of simplified lining and unlined, then black, goods engines, it was the harsh realities of railway economics that forced the new, cheaper livery for the majority of LMS locomotives.[17] Of the ex-Midland engines, only the Compounds qualified for crimson paint and the '483s' official scheme became the mixed traffic, or 'intermediate passenger livery', black with vermilion lining. Consideration had been given to using the old L&NWR lining and No. 534 was turned out in that scheme but the idea was dropped.

The entire locomotive and tender were painted black except for:

Insides of locomotive frames, weighshafts etc., axles, buffer beams and buffer housings – vermilion. Buffer beams had black edges

The lined black that became the official livery for the '483s' is shown in its early form on No. 434 at Durran Hill in April 1930. Until red-shaded transfers became available, engines were turned out with black-shaded ones that appeared to be unshaded under most conditions. Whilst this can be difficult to detect on monochrome photographs, we are convinced after close examination of this print that 434 was such a locomotive. It was in the same mechanical condition as No. 536 pictured at Nottingham, although the positioning of the tender toolboxes is a matter for conjecture under the heap of coal. This was one of the drawbacks of the separate boxes as they could become inaccessible when the tender was fully loaded.
COLLECTION R. J. ESSERY

carried over one inch onto the face.
Motion, coupling rods, buffers, couplings and hooks, whistle, opening cab window frames and some pipework – unpainted.
Inside the cab above waist level – grained oak. Inside cab roof – white.

The boiler clothing band next to the smokebox had a ½in vermilion line around the rear edge and the angle between firebox clothing and cab had the same around the front edge on the horizontal and vertical portions only (i.e., the lining stopped where the pale straw had on crimson lake engines). Vermilion lining ⅜in wide was applied as follows:

Inset about an inch from the front and lower edges of the platform angles.
Around the inside edges of the splasher beading.
Around the inside edges of the lower cab side beading.
Around the upper cab sides from the rainstrip, down the front of the upper side, along the top of the butt strip to the cut-out, and then around the cut-out and up to the rainstrip. It was inset about an inch from the front edge, cut-out beading and upper edge of the butt strip. There was none along the rainstrip.
On the inside edges of the beading on tender sides and rear with the exception of the vertical central butt strip. The top of the flare also had a continuous vermilion line about 2in below the edge on sides and rear.

A letter was issued on 18th April 1928 stating that, 'It has now been decided that three sizes of figures shall be used – 10in, 12in and 14in (14in are similar to those that have

been stocked for a considerable time).' The 14in ones were, in fact, the old Midland face whereas 10in and 12in examples were a similar but less attractive LMS version. The same letter gave instructions that the letters 'P' and 'F' be added to passenger and freight engine power classifications. On 17th June 1929 it was announced that letters and numerals would in future be supplied shaded vermilion on the right-hand side and glazed lake below (a style sometimes referred to as 'countershading') but that existing stocks of black shaded transfers were to be used up. Thus engines repainted before the new transfers were available received the imitation gold ones with black shading in various sizes. On a black background this gave the appearance of unshaded characters unless the light caught them at the right angle. From photographs taken on orthochromatic film, the difference between black and red is difficult to assess at the best of times. With light reflecting off beading or a layer of grime covering the characters it can be virtually impossible. Thus we cannot say with any certainty for many engines whether they had black or red shaded transfers. After many hours studying good quality prints, the only engines that we are prepared to state had black shaded ones with 14in numerals were Nos. 407, 411, 414,

419, 434, 444, 448, 456, 499, 502, 503 and 532. Nos. 541 and 550 may also have had them.

A few engines had different sizes of numerals. No. 409 had 12in black shaded ones whilst No. 529 received the red shaded 12in version. We also have a copy of a W.L. Good photograph of No. 546 at Gloucester on 22nd June 1928, which shows the engine in unlined black with 10in black shaded numerals. This locomotive was returned to traffic on 7th March 1928 and would thus have been repainted black with 10in numerals before the instruction to re-introduce red had taken effect.

The addition of 'P' to the power classification was indicated by a 2in high gilt letter next to the brass cab side figure fixed there since Midland days (the brass numerals were retained throughout the engines' lives unless lost or damaged when they were replaced by transfers). The ensemble looked a little odd, especially in some cases where the '2' was painted black.

In February 1936, sans serif characters were introduced. They were only used for a short time and not many engines received them. The letters were again 14in but only 10in

This is the photograph referred to in the text, showing No. 546 in plain black LMS livery with no visible lining. It was taken at Gloucester on 22nd June 1928. As discussed in the text, it was repainted before the decision to reintroduce crimson for all passenger engines had reached the paint shops. It had 10in cabside numerals and 14in tender lettering, but whether they were painted or transfers we can't say.

W. L. GOOD (2182)

Most of the visible modifications carried out by the LMS can be seen in this view of No. 394 in lined black livery. Bogie brakes and bypass valves had been removed, an exhaust steam injector fitted, 'pop' safety valves substituted for the Ramsbottom ones, and the corners of the footsteps on both engine and tender turned up. As yet, however, there were no extra washout holes in boiler or firebox clothing. As well as being obvious coming out of the smokebox, the exhaust steam pipe can be seen below the platform behind the front of the leading footstep support and between the coupled wheels below ashpan level leading to the injector underneath the left-hand side of the cab. The two snap-head rivets above the lower footstep on the front support were a result of the exhaust steam injector being fitted. The original stay from the back of the support to the frame had to be removed and a new one fitted from the support to the steam pipe. Close study of the print reveals that the letters and numbers had the vermilion and lake 'counter shading' described by some contemporary observers as being most attractive. The numerals, being 14in, were in the old Midland style. The tender was a category 4 fully modified 3,250 gallon one.

COLLECTION R. J. ESSERY

numerals were produced. Although both black and vermilion shaded ones were available, we believe that all the '483s' that received the 'block style' livery had the latter. Sans serif smokebox door plates were designed to go with the transfers, although most, but not all, existing locomotives retained the Midland scroll and serif ones. Engines we have identified as having the 1936 characters with scroll and serif plates were Nos. 370, 424, 455, 468, 525 and 534. Those receiving sans serif plates and block characters included No. 549. Block style characters were also applied to Nos. 404, 425, 454, 471 and 535 but we don't know what type of plates they carried.

Late in 1937 the scroll and serif characters were reinstated, again Midland style for the 14in ones, but the colours were changed to chrome yellow with plain vermilion shading (this was another economy measure). The sans serif smokebox door plates, however, were still being produced if replacements were required and so some engines were turned out with mixed styles the reverse of the 1936 case. Unfortunately, there were some imitation gold transfers with red shading still being used and it is extremely difficult to tell the two types apart. For that reason we have only positively identified a few engines as having yellow and red characters. Those that had them with sans serif smokebox door plates were Nos. 351, 404, 416, 458, 493, 499 and 536. A combination of red and yellow transfers with scroll and serif plates was seen on Nos. 337, 364, 418, 426, 454, 480, 490, 496, 502, 520, 525, 527, 528, 545, 557 and 561.

From about 1939, locomotives with long chimneys and tall dome casings, as described earlier, had a blue dot above the cabside numerals to denote that they were banned from working over the Northern Division because of the more restricted loading gauge. This distinction was perpetuated under BR ownership and carried through to withdrawal.

Added to all the above is the fact that, although the '483s' should all have received lined black livery between 1928 and the war years, some photographs strongly suggest that there were plain black ones

The overall appearance of a 1936 liveried engine is shown by No. 549 at Bedford in May 1937. It had a sans serif smokebox door numberplate, although very few locomotives repainted with block-style transfers received these plates. The confusion caused when long and short chimneys and high and low domes were in use has been described in the text. In this view No. 549 is seen with a long Deeley chimney and low flat-topped dome casing. Despite an attempt to rationalise the situation in 1939, different combinations were to be seen for the remainder of the engines' lives. AUTHORS' COLLECTION

The 1936 block style of letters and numbers with vermilion shading, which was only applied for a short time, is clearly illustrated in this view of No. 535 at Cricklewood taken on 7th July 1937. Although the engine appears at first glance to have been plain black, it was, in fact, lined and this view shows a 'P' next to the brass '2' on the upper cab side. H. C. CASSERLEY (14369)

(apart from 546 in 1928). With the difficulties of assessing this, for the reasons described earlier, however, we are not prepared to state categorically that such was the case (the only photographs we have in which the engines are definitely plain black are undated and could have been taken during the war). To assess every photograph we have of '483s' in the late 1920s and 1930s would be a mam-

moth and, given the state of some locomotives and/or prints, possibly impossible task, so we will content ourselves with the above examples. As we have written before, especially with these locomotives, we strongly recommend working from photographs of a particular engine at a specific time when producing a model or painting.

No. 561, seen at Patricroft in 1946, also had yellow transfers with vermilion shading but there is no lining apparent. This was the norm for engines repainted during the war. It had acquired a short Stanier chimney and low dome and so did not have the blue restriction spot on the cab sides. It also had a row of washout plugs on the firebox side and one between the handrail and the platform. The latter was set deeper than the others because, although the firebox narrowed below the boiler centreline, the clothing sides were vertical.

COOPER'S RAILWAY PHOTOGRAPHS

During the Second World War, lining was omitted when engines were repainted. All the full repaints at this time seem to have had 14in transfers. Some locomotives, however, were merely retouched rather than being fully repainted and often had the numbers and letters hand-painted in plain yellow over the existing transfers. Thus it is probable that at the end of the war there were fully lined, partially lined and unlined engines with imitation gold characters shaded black or red, yellow characters with red shading, or hand-painted characters.

Nationalisation

Most locomotives underwent little or no change to their painting, lettering and numbering when the railways were nationalised on 1st January 1948 and it was several years before they were all renumbered and painted in their final BR livery. Some were withdrawn up to 1951 without ever wearing BR numbers (see Appendix B). The first alteration for many was simply that the BR number, which was the LMS number with 40,000 added to it, was applied to the cab sides in unshaded 10in LMS style scroll and serif numerals. Red shading on the tender lettering, which was usually retained, was painted over in black. Close study of photographs suggests that some of the locomotives, e.g., 40539, had the numbers painted on in the LMS

One of the engines that received the 'M' prefix to its LMS number was 436, seen in this view at Derby in July 1948. The 12in numerals were in the 1946 style without any maroon edging and all the characters were cream. The smokebox door numberplate had LMS scroll and serif numerals. Stanier chimney, low dome cover and rain gutters all feature, but the splashers were still flush riveted. There were washout plugs above the handrail. H. C. CASSERLEY (54738)

transfer style. Smokebox doors were fitted with sans serif number plates, although some engines merely had the number hand-painted on the doors for a time or carried no number at all until the plates were made. Locomotives could be seen in this state for some time, some right up to withdrawal in the early 1950s.

A minority, e.g., Nos. 436 and 536, received the short-lived M prefix to their LMS numbers. In these cases the pale cream characters were in the same style as the 1946 LMS livery without the maroon embellishment, the sans serif 'M' being 8in high and the numerals 12in. Tenders of these engines had 'BRITISH RAILWAYS' in matching style 10in letters on their sides. Unlike other classes that received this livery, the '483s' do not seem to have had the prefix added to the smokebox door plates. No. 436 carried a serif plate at this time whilst 536's was sans serif.

There were some hybrids of the above liveries. For example, due to a tender change, No. 40402 had its number on the cab sides in 10in LMS transfers and carried a BR smokebox door plate but 'BRITISH RAILWAYS' in 10in cream letters was on the tender. Conversely, No. 40556 had 1946 pattern straw numerals on the cab with 'LMS' on its tender, the numerals being higher up than usual only about 10in below the butt strip. When photographed in this condition on 22nd June 1950 it was without a smokebox door number plate.

The scheme decided on in 1948 for mixed traffic and lesser passenger locomotives was based on the pre-Grouping L&NWR passenger livery. The entire engine and tender, inside and out, was painted black except for:

Buffer housings, beams and the portions of vacuum stand pipes next to them – signal red.
Buffers, couplings and hooks, motion and whistle – unpainted.
Inside of cab roof – white.

On 10th July 1948 No. 40562 was photographed at Derby in fairly typical condition for a '483' immediately following nationalisation. The new BR number had been applied in unshaded LMS style 10in numerals on a repainted cab side. A small area had been touched up for the application of a fresh 'P' behind the brass '2' of the power class and the shading on the LMS lettering of the tender had been painted over. The locomotive had a short Stanier chimney, low dome casing and a 'full set' of washout plugs on the firebox. Snap-head rivets had been used during repairs to the splashers and rain gutters had been welded to the eaves of the cab. It did not have an exhaust steam injector. Filthy and with steam leaking freely, it makes a sorry sight.
COLLECTION R. J. ESSERY

A rare variation in livery was this example at Crewe North in March 1953. No. 40332 had 10in plain 1946 style numerals and a BR Derby/Bow works smokebox door numberplate. The power class was still shown (just) in brass '2' and transfer 'P' on the upper cab side. The tender was category 2 with short side plate extensions.
COLLECTION R. J. ESSERY

The first version of the lined BR black paint scheme had 'BRITISH RAILWAYS' on the tender tank in 10in cream letters. The cabside numerals were 8in high and the power class just above them. No. 40439 was at Aschurch with a Redditch branch train when this picture was taken in 1949 and shows that the scheme looked quite good on the '483s' when fairly recently painted and clean. The original print shows that the brass '2' was still on the upper cab side and had been polished, even though '2P' was below the butt strip. Once again, the engine did not have an exhaust steam injector.
J. H. MOSS

Two types of lining were used. Splasher sides, lower cab sides and tender sides had panels of multi-coloured lining, the outside edge inset 5in from the panel edge, with 90 degree corners being 4in external radius. Corners and curves on the splashers did not, as far as we know, have specified radii but just followed the shape of the panel. Going from the outside, the lining was ⅝in pale grey, ⅛in cream, 1⅝in black and ¼in red. Whilst that was the official layout, it is possible that some engines had the lining set closer to the edges of the cab and tender sides and that the black line between cream and grey was narrower than specified. On the platform angles, the lower edges were grey with cream above and the red lines were halfway up the angle. Boiler and cylinder clothing bands were edged with ¼in red lines.

Locomotive running numbers were on the cab sides in 8in cream Gill Sans numerals with the power classification immediately above in the same style. Many engines still had the old Midland brass '2s' in front of the cab cut-outs but, if present, they were normally painted over. The blue spot indicative of engines precluded from the former Northern Division and a few other lines was, if applicable, above the power class on the lower cab side. Raised, white painted numerals were also used on cast smokebox door plates in a sans serif style that was peculiar to Derby and Bow Works. Comparison with the cabside numerals will illustrate the different faces. Raised characters and

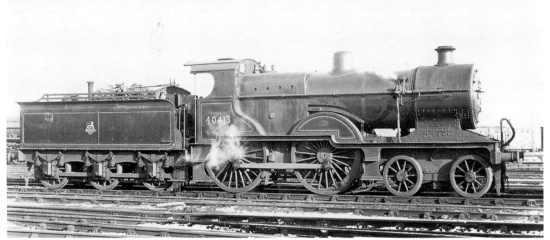

A few locomotives had their fluted coupling rods replaced with plain rectangular section Stanier ones. No. 40413, photographed at Crewe North in January 1953, was one of them. It had the lined BR livery with the first style of emblem to the rear of the centre butt strip. Other details were by then fairly standard and have been commented on in other pictures.

REAL PHOTOGRAPHS

No. 40553's last recorded tender change was in January 1952 when it got a 3,500 gallon one that had been originally built for a Class 4 goods engine. As can be seen here, although the engine was in lined BR mixed traffic livery, the tender was unlined. The brass '2' was still on the cab side, albeit painted over, and there was a cover on the lower washout hole. It had a washout plug in the front ring of the boiler just below the handrail. No. 40553 did not have an exhaust steam injector.
AUTHORS' COLLECTION

borders on shed code plates, tender number plates and capacity plates were white. In the early days of this scheme, some tenders had 'BRITISH RAILWAYS' on the sides, again in cream Gill Sans 10in characters. Fairly soon, however, the smaller size of the early BR emblem with a lion astride a wheel was placed within the lining panel, immediately to the rear of the centre butt strip. We have no evidence of any *lined* '483s' with the 1956 coat of arms.

Although lined black was the usual and, we believe, official livery for the '483s' under nationalisation, quite a few of them appeared in plain black right up to 1962. Some, such as Nos. 40413, 40440, 40425, 40447, 40509, 40519 and 40520, were photographed as late as 1954 without any visible markings on their tenders either (40413 having plain coupling rods and an ex-Class 4 goods 3,500 gallon tender at the time) but with standard cabside numbers and power class figures.

Even with the first BR lion-on-wheel emblem on the tenders, there were instances of plain black locomotives. Nos. 40356, 40362, 40407, 40409, 40421, 40426, 40452, 40453, 40454, 40480, 40485, 40486, 40495, 40501, 40502 and 40536 were all seen in this condition between 1950 and 1962 whilst coupled to 'original 483' tenders. Additionally, Nos. 40453, 40487, 40511, and 40540 in plain black had 'standard' 3,500 gallon tenders, and 40461 and 40536 had ex Class 4 goods ones.

Finally, the only three '483s' we know of that had the post-1956 coat of arms on their tenders were all plain black. In May 1957 No. 40557 was seen at Derby coupled to one of the usual '483' type 3,500 gallon Johnson tenders with separate toolboxes, angled side plate extensions and frame-mounted footsteps, No. 40504 was photographed at Kentish Town in May 1958 with a beaded, LMS 'standard' 3,500 gallon tender without coal rails, and a year later No. 40537 was at Templecombe attached to the same type of tender with coal rails. Further details of the locomotive/tender combinations referred to above are in the tender section and Appendix D.

Although lined black was the official paint scheme after 1948, there were engines such as No. 40453 that had no lining. In October 1956 it was attached to an LMS standard 3,500 gallon tender, as seen in this picture. As well as these distinctions, 40453 was one of the few engines to have had plain coupling rods and was one of the last three '483s' withdrawn in 1962. Except for the tender and rods, it was in fairly normal condition for one of its class when photographed at Derby in 1956 with Stanier chimney, low dome casing, extra washout holes (the lower one having a cover) and snap-headed rivets all over the place.
COLLECTION R. J. ESSERY

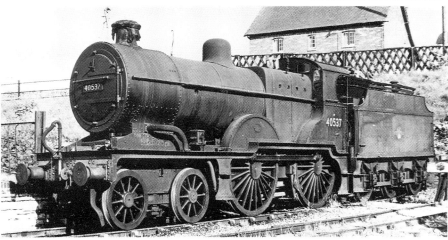

Although one of the last three withdrawals in 1962, No. 40537 was out of use when this picture was taken at Templecombe in May 1959 and the makers' plate had been removed from its splasher. As with all the other instances we know of when the 1956 BR coat of arms was applied, the locomotive and tender were plain black. The tender, which had coal rails, was one of those built with a 3,500 gallon tank on Johnson 2,950 gallon frames and was originally coupled to LMS Compound No. 1111. The engine had a washout plug in the front ring of the boiler and was in the all too usual 1950s condition of filthy neglect.
COLLECTION R. J. ESSERY

POSTSCRIPT

When first introduced, the '483s' were an important element of the Midland's passenger engine stock. Although not top-flight engines in Grouping and BR days, they filled an important niche and actually outlived many of their more glamorous contemporaries. Withdrawal began immediately following nationalisation and by the end of 1948 Nos. 408, 492, 494 and 545 had gone. The class was far from moribund at that stage, however, and was still undergoing modification as described earlier. The middle 1950s saw large numbers taken out of service and by the beginning of 1956 less than half remained. The last one working was 40537 but the last in stock was 40453, which was withdrawn in September 1962. Not only was it the last '483' in stock, it was the last Midland Railway 4–4–0. Built in 1894 in the Derby batch of '2203' Class engines, it was renewed in 1920 to O/4476. Sadly, no-one saw fit to preserve it, nor any of its brethren, which is a shame considering the amount of revenue these attractive locomotives must have earned for the Midland, LMS and British Railways in their 50 years of service.

APPENDICES
APPENDIX A – PAINTING DETAILS

As well as describing the livery details for the engines in this series of books, we are attempting, mainly for the benefit of modellers and artists, to summarise wherever possible the painting methods used. Unfortunately, we do not have a specification for Midland or LMS passenger engines during the period in which the '483s' were painted crimson lake. The only two we do have are from the turn of the century and 1935, which neatly bracket what is required! Midland or LMS crimson lake is a notoriously difficult colour to define and there have been many pages of print devoted to it. For detailed discussions on the subject we would refer readers to two works – *An Illustrated Review of Midland Locomotives Volume 1* published by Wild Swan in 1984 and *An Illustrated History of LMS Locomotives Volume 1* published by Oxford Publishing Co. in 1981 reprinted 1988, both by Essery and Jenkinson. The bottom line, as the saying goes, is that the undercoat and varnishing of a crimson lake finish is important to the final appearance of the colour, as crimson lake itself is a relatively translucent pigment.

Although we don't have a specification from the 1912 to 1928 period, a comparison of the 1900 and 1935 ones suggest that there were only a few differences in the intervening years. Unfortunately, the Midland one refers to paints as being 'to sample supplied' rather than specifying the colour, but there are several reasons to suppose that the pre- and post-Grouping colours were virtually the same. It was, after all, the Midland influence in the early days of the Grouping that led to its adoption and in 1923 a Derby works order referred to the crimson lake as 'Midland colour'. Orders connected with the 'Royal Scots' in 1927 describe the nameplates and splashers as being 'Derby Red' and the term 'Midland red' was used in relation to the 'Princess Royals'.

The 1900 Midland specification basically required that the crimson areas be given two coats of oxide of iron paint followed by two coats of 'oxide and lake', lining and transfers applied and finished with three coats of varnish rubbed down between each. Inside the frames and the axles received two coats of oxide of iron, one of vermilion and two of varnish. All black areas had one coat of black and one of Japan (a glossy black lacquer). Inside the cab above waist level there were two coats of oxide of iron followed by one of 'light oak graining colour' and three of varnish. Buffer beams were given one coat of vermilion, transfers applied and finished with three coats of varnish.

The more detailed 1935 LMS schedule can be summarised as follows. The insides of the frames and the axles on the locomotive were given one coat of bauxite, one of vermilion and a final coat of vermilion mixed 50/50 with varnish. All other external areas and the inside of the cab were given two coats of red oxide steel primer, rubbed down between coats. Crimson areas were given one application of 'brown undercoat' followed by a coat of 'standard crimson lake'. The former was a mixture of red oxide of iron and varnish (in a ratio of approximately 4:1) with a little turpentine and liquid drier added. The main colour was lake paste and varnish in a 3:1 ratio, again with the addition of turpentine and liquid drier. The black edging was put on followed by a coat of varnish, lining and transfers and two more coats of varnish, with the surface flattened between coats. Buffer beams were given two coats of vermilion, the edging and lining applied and finished with two coats of varnish. Black areas were mainly painted with 'common black', which was black pigment and dark gold size in linseed oil and white spirit with liquid drier added. Smokeboxes also received a coat of black enamel.

It would seem, therefore, that the only practical differences between the two methods were that the Midland applied two coats of the main colour to the LMS's one and whereas the Midland specification refers to 'oxide and lake', the LMS stipulated paint in which only lake paste was the coloration. We would not wish to judge whether this in fact produced a different final colour, but once again would point out that, as far as the LMS was concerned, post-Grouping engines were 'Midland Red'. The statement we have sometimes heard that LMS locomotives had a less glossy finish does not seem borne out as both regimes stipulated that three coats of varnish be applied over the main colour (although it is arguable that the different specifications would have given Midland engines a glossier finish in the black areas). It is far more likely that cleaning was more often and assiduously undertaken before the 1914–18 war. Photographs of crimson LMS engines in ex-works condition show a superb gloss finish that appears to be the equal of Midland locomotives.

In *Midland Engines No. 2* we gave details of the LMS painting schedule for black locomotives issued in 1935. The schedule for the lined black livery in which the '483s' were painted was the same except that vermilion lining was added before the second coat of varnish was applied over the black.

APPENDIX B – REBUILDING AND WITHDRAWAL DATES

TABLE 1 – REBUILDING DATES
All rebuilt from H boilered condition. Information taken from Midland locomotive register.

Date	Locomotives rebuilt
1912	483, 486–488, 490, 492–497, 500–510, 512–516, 518, 520, 522 (No. 494 was the first to be rebuilt)
1913	484*, 485, 489, 491, 498, 499, 511, 517, 519, 521, 525–530, 532–537, 539, 541–543, 546, 548, 549, 551, 552, 554–556, 558, 560–562
1914	405–408, 412, 414–416, 418, 424, 425, 436, 437, 444, 464, 466, 482, 524, 531, 538, 540, 544, 545, 547, 553, 557, 559
1915	427, 433, 443, 458, 461, 463, 523, 550
1916	420, 426, 432, 434, 455, 462, 468
1917	417, 453, 470, 479
1918	404, 411, 413, 421, 423
1919	409, 419, 448
1920	403, 447, 452, 456
1921	410, 430, 446
1922	370, 395, 397, 400–402, 422, 454, 459, 471, 477, 478, 480
1923	332, 337, 351, 353, 356, 359, 362, 377, 394, 396, 438, 439, 450, 472
1924	364

*As first rebuilt to '483' Class, No. 484 had a G7 saturated boiler but in 1914 it was replaced with a G7S.

TABLE 2 – WITHDRAWAL DATES
*indicates withdrawal before BR number applied. Information taken from locomotive history cards except for Nos. 408, 40492, 494 and 545 whose cards are missing. Dates for these engines were taken from a secondary source that we believe to be correct.

Date	Locomotives Withdrawn
1948	408*, 492*, 494*, 545*
1949	394*, 400*, 437*, 456*, 40459, 466*, 479*, 483*, 496*, 40500, 506*, 510*, 517*, 544*, 554*, 555*
1950	403*, 40427, 446*, 468*, 40478, 40488, 490*, 40498, 512*, 40515, 40516, 40533, 561*
1951	40370, 40397, 406*, 40424, 40462, 40470, 40477, 40497, 40508, 530*, 40546, 549*
1952	40415, 40417, 40423, 40430, 40471, 40499, 40503, 40507, 40514, 40523, 40528, 40532, 40558, 40560
1953	40351, 40353, 40401, 40410, 40422, 40425, 40432, 40444, 40484, 40505, 40547, 40551
1954	40359, 40395, 40436, 40438, 40455, 40480, 40524, 40529, 40539
1955	40377, 40405, 40419, 40448, 40472, 40522, 40535, 40562
1956	40362, 40364, 40434, 40463, 40518, 40521, 40526, 40527, 40531, 40556
1957	40356, 40404, 40409, 40414, 40418, 40426, 40433, 40450, 40458, 40482, 40485, 40486, 40495, 40509, 40519, 40520, 40525, 40559
1958	40337, 40407, 40420, 40447, 40464, 40541, 40553
1959	40332, 40412, 40413, 40416, 40461, 40493, 40513, 40534, 40536, 40538, 40542, 40550
1960	40402, 40454, 40489, 40491, 40501, 40552
1961	40396, 40411, 40421, 40439, 40443, 40452, 40487, 40502, 40504, 40511, 40543, 40548, 40557
1962	40453, 40537, 40540

APPENDIX C – DISTRICT AND SHED ALLOCATIONS

When referring to these lists it should be remembered that locomotives were sometimes reallocated quite frequently, occasionally remaining at a shed for only a few weeks before moving on, whereas at other times they remained at one shed for many years. To reproduce the movements of every engine throughout its lifetime would require a book in itself and so we have taken five dates for which we have provided 'snapshots' of the Class 2 distribution over a 36 year period. This means that some locations, referred to at the end of the tables, are recorded in the engine history cards as having had superheater Class 2s for a time but are not here represented. The dates for the tables have been chosen for two reasons. Firstly, we have picked dates for which we have reliable information from allocation lists, stock books and engine history cards. Secondly, we have borne in mind the modelling fraternity (which includes us!) and tried to choose dates that correspond with popular periods for steam railway modellers. The source we have used for the pre-Grouping period is the Midland allocation list for November 1920. Early post-Grouping days, when the '483s' wore LMS crimson lake livery, are represented by the 1st January 1927 list taken from the first entries in the engine history cards. From those cards, cross-referred to the 1944 LMS stock book, we have taken the beginning of 1935 to fit in with the popular pre-war Grouping era. The 1944 list is taken from the LMS stock book. We intended to produce a list for 1948 to coincide with nationalisation and the beginning of British Railways, but the number of anomalies we found in the engine history cards effectively precluded it. Our final list, 1st January 1956, represents a very popular period when there were still an appreciable number of the '483s' left in service. There are some caveats explained with the individual lists but we hope that the information given will prove useful and interesting.

TABLE 3 – 1ST NOVEMBER 1920
This table has been compiled from a Midland Railway list and gives district rather than individual shed allocations. For an explanation of Midland district and shed organisation we would refer readers to *LMS Engine Sheds Volume 2* by Chris Hawkins and George Reeve published by Wild Swan in 1981. This series of books is an invaluable source of information for those interested in LMS and constituent companies' locomotive stabling and servicing arrangements.

District	Locomotives Allocated
Bedford	461, 462, 533–535, 551–556
Birmingham	405, 505, 507–512, 514, 515
Bristol	426, 506, 513, 516–527, 531
Carlisle	432–434, 436–437, 443, 444, 458, 463, 468
Derby	488–504
Gloucester	414, 420, 466
Kentish Town	419, 528, 548, 557–559, 562
Lancaster	448, 452, 453, 455, 456
Leeds	479, 482
Leicester	529, 530, 532, 536–547, 549, 550, 561
Manchester	447
Nottingham	404, 406–409, 411, 415–418, 421, 423–425, 427, 483–487, 560
Sheffield	412, 413
Skipton	464, 470

No. 403, listed in Table 1 as being renewed in 1920, was not completed until December after the allocation list referred to was issued.

TABLE 4 – 1ST JANUARY 1927
This table, compiled from the engine history cards, again gives the old Midland district rather than sub-shed allocations. In the case of Birmingham, however, we know that the shed in question was Saltley. Generally the engines were still based at ex-Midland sheds so Carlisle refers to Durran Hill. Again we would refer readers to *LMS Engine Sheds Volume 2* for more details.

We have no positive information on the four locomotives withdrawn in 1948, Nos. 408, 492, 494 or 545, for this date as their his-

tory cards were not preserved. The first one mentioned was in the middle of a block allocated to Nottingham that had all been there in 1920 and hadn't moved. The same applied to 492 and 494 at Derby and 545 was in a similar situation at Leicester. We feel that this probably indicates their whereabouts.

Date	Locomotives allocated
Bedford	461, 462, 548–54
Birmingham (Saltley)	430, 437–9, 505, 507–13
Bristol	414, 420, 426, 506, 514–529
Burton	377
Buxton	332, 459
Carlisle	432–4, 436, 443, 444, 446, 463, 468
Derby	488–491, 493, 495–504
Hasland	370
Kentish Town	419, 487, 555–562
Leeds	362, 364, 477–480, 482–484
Leicester	530–544, 546, 547
Manchester	351, 353, 356, 447, 466, 485, 486
Nottingham	403–7, 409–11, 415–18, 421–5, 427
Sheffield	337, 359, 394, 412, 413, 458
Skipton	448, 450, 452–6, 464, 470–2
Worcester	395–7
York	400–2

Locations not listed above that are recorded as having '483s' in the 1920s were Liverpool, Kettering and Shoeburyness.

TABLE 5 – 1ST JANUARY 1935
The reorganisation of LMS sheds under the 'Motive Power Area Locomotive Supply, Repair, Concentration and Garage Scheme', inaugurated in 1933, was in full swing in 1935. It was aimed at improving the overall efficiency of locomotive working and involved, amongst other things, remodelling track layouts and providing new handling and maintenance facilities at many sheds. It also meant that the administrative structure of districts and sheds was altered and some sheds closed. This inevitably led to some confusion and there are anomalies in the engine history cards, such as the inclusion of both districts and individual sheds. As an example, Birmingham, which was a district, is given as a location, as are Saltley, a main or concentration depot within that district, and the garage depot, or sub-shed, of Bournville. We have managed to clear up some of these anomalies but there are still some engines for which we can only give district allocations. In order to give an idea of the distribution of the '483s' in the mid-1930s, however, we are including the list here. Once again, Carlisle refers to Durran Hill, which was to close in February 1936. More details of the LMS reorganisation can be found in *LMS Engine Sheds Volume 1*.

Since the engine history cards for Nos. 408, 492, 494 and 545 are missing, they are not included (the LMS stock book issued in April 1944 gives their locations as Peterborough, Crewe North, Rhyl and Rowsley respectively).

District/Shed	Locomotives Allocated
Bath	531
Bedford	461, 549–554
Belle Vue	514
Birmingham	397, 517
Bournville	439
Bradford	479, 483
Bristol	518, 520, 522–4
Burton	377
Buxton	332, 403, 413, 447, 448, 462, 489
Carlisle	432–4, 436, 444, 446, 463, 468
Derby	495, 497–504, 516, 525, 526
Gloucester	395, 519, 521, 527–30
Grimesthorpe	534
Hasland	337, 359, 364, 370, 414, 466, 490, 491, 493, 506
Kettering	426, 548
Kentish Town	555–562
Lancaster	450, 452–6

District/Shed	Locomotives Allocated
Leeds	480, 482, 484, 488, 547
Leicester	530, 535–544
Longsight	356
Manchester	515
Nottingham	404–7, 409–11, 415–425, 427, 430, 437, 438, 496
Peterborough	532, 533
Saltley	396, 486, 505, 507–13
Sheffield	351, 353, 362, 394, 400, 412, 443, 477, 478, 485, 487, 546
Skipton	458, 459, 470–2
York	401, 402

Other locations recorded as having '483s' in the 1930s were Abergavenny, Birkenhead, Bletchley, Bushbury, Camden, Canklow, Chester, Hellifield, Llandudno Junction, Millhouses, Shrewsbury, Staveley, Templecombe, Warwick and Workington.

TABLE 6 – 8TH APRIL 1944

This table has been compiled using the LMS stock book of that date.

Shed	Locomotives Allocated
Bedford	551
Bournville	439, 517
Bristol	497, 499
Burton	364, 395, 500, 525
Buxton	438
Camden	425
Canklow	485
Chester	446, 479, 508, 524
Coalville	541
Crewe North	397, 471, 492, 529
Crewe South	402, 405, 448
Derby	406, 407, 418, 513, 516, 326
Gloucester	409, 423, 437
Hasland	337, 370, 466, 490, 491, 506, 555–7
Heaton Mersey	453, 544
Hellifield	456, 459, 470, 472
Kentish Town	477, 547
Kettering	454, 537, 550
Lancaster	353, 488
Leeds	426, 432, 436, 455, 458, 482, 489, 519, 558, 562
Leicester	535, 542, 543, 549, 552, 553
Llandudno Jct.	396, 413, 495
Longsight	403, 531, 539
Mansfield	424, 503
Millhouses	400, 422, 487, 546
Normanton	480, 521
Northampton	412, 421, 430
Nottingham	404, 411, 415–7, 419, 427, 496, 498, 502, 504, 559, 560
Nuneaton	510, 522
Patricroft	332, 377, 527, 507, 528
Peterborough	408, 410, 532, 533
Preston	356, 483
Rhyl	494
Rowsley	394, 478, 523, 530, 545
Royston	444, 514
Rugby	420, 433, 450, 464, 534, 554
Saltley	463, 486, 493, 505, 509, 511, 512, 518
Sheffield	362, 401, 468, 520
Skipton	351, 359, 452, 484
Springs Branch	447, 561
Stafford	443, 461
Walsall	462, 501, 515
Westhouses	414
Wellingborough	536, 538, 540, 548
Willesden	434

Other locations recorded as having had '483s' in the 1940s were Aston, Bangor, Bath, Bletchley, Brunswick, Carlisle, Denbigh, Edge Hill, Kirkby, Monument Lane, Shrewsbury, Templecombe, Toton, Trafford Park and Warrington.

TABLE 7 – 1ST JANUARY 1956

This table has been compiled from the engine history cards.

Shed	Locomotives Allocated
Bournville	40439, 40463
Bristol	40426, 40486
Burton	40364, 40453, 40519, 40525, 40526
Carlisle	40396, 40412, 40536
Chester	40559
Crewe North	40332, 40413, 40447
Derby	40356, 40404, 40407, 40416, 40418, 40513
Gloucester	40489, 40540, 40541
Hasland	40337, 40491, 40502, 40537, 40550, 40556, 40557
Heaton Mersey	40433
Lancaster	40362
Leeds	40518
Leicester	40402, 40452, 40485, 40542, 40543
Llandudno Jct.	40548
Longsight	40482
Manningham	40552
Millhouses	40538
Northampton	40421, 40464, 40534
Nottingham	40411, 40454, 40458, 40487, 40493, 40504, 40553
Patricroft	40434, 40450
Preston	40420
Rhyl	40495
Rowsley	40520
Royston	40521
Saltley	40511
Skipton	40409, 40414
Stafford	40443, 40461
Templecombe	40509
Walsall	40501, 40531
Widnes	40527

Other locations recorded as having '483s' in the 1950s were Bedford, Brunswick, Kentish Town, Mansfield, Peterborough, Tebay and Toton.

APPENDIX D -TENDER ALLOCATIONS FROM *CIRCA* JANUARY 1928

Midland Railway tenders carried the same number as the locomotive to which they were attached. On 24th January 1928 a list of distinctive tender numbers for the Midland Division was issued. This table was prepared using the engine history cards, which purport to show tender numbers from 1st January 1927 although it may be that the recording of numbers was later than that, hence the tentative commencement date. Replacement 3,500 gallon tenders are referred to as follows:

'3,500 gallon' – Johnson type as fitted to the '483s' when rebuilt.
'Class 4' – originally attached to Class 4 goods engines.
'Belpaire' – ex-Johnson '700' Class.
'bogie' – Deeley rebuilt bogie tender.
'990' – ex-Deeley '990' Class.
'hybrid' – 3,500 gallon tank on Johnson 2,950 gallon frames.
'LMS standard' – straight-sided Fowler type.

Further details of these tenders are given on page **31.** Only Midland/LMS locomotive numbers are given in the table for simplicity.

Engine Nos.	Tender Nos.	Remarks
332	1912	3,250 gallon
337	1915	3,250 gallon
		2719 (3,500 gallon) attached 10/53

Engine Nos.	Tender Nos.	Remarks	Engine Nos.	Tender Nos.	Remarks
351, 353, 356	1923–1925	3,250 gallon 356 got 2729 (3,500 gallon) in 12/31	466, 468, 470–472, 477–480, 482, 483–522, 549	2015–2065	3,250 gallon 477 got 1938 in 9/35; 484 got 2038 in 12/33 (both 3,250 gallon). 487 got 4107 in 9/56 (LMS standard). 488 got 2792 in 12/31 (Belpaire). 489 got 2874 in 1/58 (hybrid). 490 got 1998 in 12/31 (3,250 gallon). 491 got 4456 in 11/57 (LMS standard), 493 got 1970 in 5/54; 496 got 1966 in 12/32; 497 got 1949 in 2/37, 501 got 1895 in 12/31 (all 3,250 gallon). 503 got 2723 in 12/31 (3,500 gallon). 504 got 3712 in 11/55 (LMS standard). 511 got 3536 in 11/57 (hybrid). 516 got 2043 in 12/31; 519 got 1988 in 4/52 (both 3,250 gallon). 520 got 2807 in 6/29 (990). 521 got 2052 in 8/49; 549 got 1918 in 12/31. (both 3,250 gallon)
359	1927	3,250			
362	1929	3,250 gallon			
364	1931	3,250 gallon			
370	1936	3,250 gallon			
377	1940	3,250 gallon			
394–397	1956–1959	3,250 gallon 394 got 1979 (3,250 gallon) in 10/36			
400–416	1960–1976	3,250 gallon 401 got 2710 in 7/48 (3,500 gallon). 402 got 2992 in 7/51 (Class 4). 404 got 1969 in 12/32 and 1980 in 10/52 (both 3,250 gallon). 407 got 1977 in 10/35 and 1967 in 1/36 (both 3,250 gallon) and 3715 in 10/56 (LMS standard). 409 got 1933 in 12/31, then 1956 in 10/36 and 2016 in 5/56; 411 got 1939 in 12/36; 412 got 2015 in 3/49 (all 3,250 gallon). 413 got 3073 in 8/54 (Class 4) and 416 got 4108 in 5/56 (LMS standard)	523–548, 550–562	2692–2730	3,500 gallon 524 got 1978 in 12/32; 525 got 2054 in 2/50; 526 got 1971 in 7/38 (all 3,250 gallon). 529 got 1999 in 2/42 (3,500 gallon) and 1999 in 12/43 (3,250 gallon). 531 got 1991 in 8/54; 534 got 1910 in 12/33; 535 got 1970 in 3/54 then 2035 in 5/54 (all 3,250 gallon). 536 got 3026 in 11/54 (Class 4). 537 got 3535 in 5/55 (hybrid) and 2008 by 4/62 (3,250 gallon). 538 got 1924 in 8/53 (3,250 gallon). 540 got 2008 in 1/50 (3,250 gallon) then 3236 date unknown (LMS standard). 541 got 1961 in 7/48 (3,250 gallon). 542 got 2768 in 4/55 (bogie). 548 got 2762 in 12/31 and 2763 in 12/32 (both bogie) then 1997 in 8/49 and 1992 in 9/54 (both 3,250 gallon). 552 got 2000 in 1935 (3,250 gallon). 553 got 2788 in 12/31 (Belpaire) and 3036 in 1/52 (Class 4). 555 got 2797 in 12/31 (Belpaire). 557 got 2787 in 12/31 (Belpaire) then 1983 in 10/52 (3,250 gallon). 559 got 2874 in 8/54 (hybrid). 561 got 2058 in 12/31 (3,250 gallon)
417–427, 430, 432–434, 436–439, 443, 444, 446–448, 450, 452–456, 458, 459	1977–2008	3,250 gallon 417 got 1967 in 10/35 and 1977 in 1/36; 418 got 1964 in 12/32,1980 in 3/35 and 1969 in 10/52; 419 got 1951 in 6/36; 420 got 2026 in 12/33 (all 3,250 gallon). 421 got 2865 in 3/58 (hybrid). 422 got 2034 in 1/49 (3,250 gallon). 434 got 2693 in 12/33 (3,500 gallon) and 1917 in 2/37 (3,250 gallon). 438 got 1991 in 4/34; 444 got 1941 in 4/48; 446 got 2003 in 12/31 (all 3,250 gallon). 447 got 2698 in 2/42 (3,500 gallon) then 1999 in 12/42 (3,250 gallon), 2698 in 12/43 (3,500 gallon) and 1989 in 1/54 (3,250 gallon). 448 got 1964 in 4/35 and 2036 in 5/40; 452 got 2056 in 1/52 (all 3,250 gallon). 453 got 1903 in 12/31 (3,250 gallon) and 4400 in 10/56 (LMS standard). 454 got 2717 in 12/31 (3,500 gallon) and 1923 in 12/53 (3,250 gallon). 455 got 2778 in 12/31 (Belpaire) and 2009 in 10/35 (3,250 gallon)			
461–464	2010–2013	3,250 gallon 461 got 3061 in 12/54 (Class 4) and 462 got 1964 in 1/49 (3,250 gallon)			

NOTES IN TEXT

1. This total excludes the five S&DJR '483' Class engines that were numbered 322–326 when they were taken into LMS stock in 1930. There were three other S&DJR superheated 4–4–0s, which were standard 2P types built in 1928 as LMS Nos. 575, 576 and 580 before being sold to the joint line.

2. Within the generic term 'H boilers' we are including H1 and HX units. Although heating surfaces, tube arrangements and firebox construction varied, they had the same external dimensions. Further details can be found in *Midland Engines No. 2*.

3. There were some larger Midland locomotives schemed out in Johnson's time. One of them, an outside-cylindered 0–8–0, was approved for construction and ten were ordered but they were cancelled soon after Johnson left. An article on proposed Midland 8-coupled engines and the S&DJR 2–8–0s by Phil Atkins appeared in *Midland Record No. 13*.

4. For some good background reading on iron girder bridge design and development see articles by Keith Horne in volumes 11 and 13 of *Backtrack* published by Atlantic Publishers. The fact that Midland Locomotive Superintendents/CMEs tried to get larger designs approved seems rather odd if they knew that their plans would be rejected. This seems to suggest one of three possibilities: that they didn't know what they were doing or chose to ignore the restrictions, which is patently ridiculous; that they anticipated an easing of the restrictions due to hoped-for improvements in the civil engineering; or that they were working in the dark without knowing accurately what the restrictions were. We offer no answer of our own to this, but it may be instructive to paraphrase remarks made by E.S. Cox when describing the process of scheming out engines on the L&YR and in the early days of the LMS. He wrote that proposals could be rejected because they did not satisfy the bridge loading restrictions without any details being given. Thus locomotive designers were not only hamstrung but had virtually to work in the dark, hoping that their schemes would somehow meet with approval. Their only

guidelines were what had been accepted previously. This patently ridiculous state of affairs persisted until Stanier 'called the bluff' of the civil engineers and insisted on proper studies being undertaken. The result was that many of the previously inviolate rules were found to be quite unnecessary.

5. As far as official Midland Railway terminology was concerned, an engine was only 'rebuilt' if it got a new boiler in the process. If it didn't it wasn't rebuilt, even if it underwent fairly major alteration.

6. The potential advantages of superheating had been recognised in the late 1820s by Trevithick and by the Stephensons and others in the 1830s, The problem of lubrication with dry steam, however, meant that they weren't really viable for a long time. Successful superheating was first applied to stationary engines, one of the engineers involved being Dr. Wilhelm Schmidt. He turned his attentions to locomotives in the late 1890s and the first Schmidt superheaters were used on the Prussian State Railways in 1897. Aspinall tried a system of his own on some Atlantics in 1899 but it was the later type of Schmidt superheater, having boiler flues containing the superheater elements and first used by Flamme in Belgium in 1901, that was widely adopted in the early part of the 20th century.

7. There is no doubt that the Midland intended eventually to rebuild the whole series from 328 to 562 as '483' Class superheated engines. The Orders list those to be rebuilt roughly in their 'slim-boilered' class groupings and there are no gaps in the sequence. By 1921, however, the number of engines authorised was being reduced.

8. The system of alphabetic nomenclature for boiler types was started by Johnson shortly after he became Locomotive Superintendent. When the letter 'G' was reached, it happened to coincide with the introduction of Belpaire boilers and from then on 'G' indicated a boiler with a Belpaire firebox. The number was the nominal firebox length, so 'G7' meant a boiler having a 7ft long Belpaire firebox. When superheating was adopted, it was shown by an 'S'. An 'X' indicated that the boiler was different in some way from the main group, e.g., HX boilers had different arrangements of back plate fittings and valve mountings whereas G7X was the designation for G7 boilers with steel inner fireboxes. 'A' and 'B' were used to sub-divide otherwise closely similar boilers, such as the G9 of the Deeley Compounds and the G9A of the '900' Class, which differed in tubes, tubeplates and mud holes. The system was carried on into the LMS but started to get a bit unwieldy. Such designations as G10½S for the 'Royal Scots' or G9HS (the 'H' indicating Horwich) for the parallel-boilered 2-6-0s were used. When Stanier took over he introduced his own system for new boilers but left the old designations in place.

9. The heating surfaces quoted are taken from a table prepared in 1919. By that time figures were being calculated according to a formula agreed on by the Association of Railway Locomotive Engineers in November 1914. Before then there was no common method of producing them, even within one company, and so figures may have varied depending on the source.

10. Most Midland Railway locomotives were right-hand drive whereas the LMS standard became left-hand drive. Thus the Midland G7S types – '483s', 0-6-4Ts and Class 4 goods engines – differed from the later LMS standard G7S engines. When the latter were first introduced, their boilers had firebox back plates and front boiler barrel rings fitted only for left-hand drive. After a short while, however, (we don't know exactly how long) they were arranged so that either layout was possible and the unused fixing holes blanked off. Thus they became interchangeable between all classes.

11. The positioning of the valves under inside cylinders almost inevitably led to constricted steam passages. Outside cylinders gave designers more freedom to incorporate large, straight passages but the Midland generally preferred to stick to inside ones, possibly because of the relatively restricted loading gauge (a scheme to rebuild the '483s' with 20in outside cylinders was considered in the mid-1920s but rejected). Slide valves could be mounted between inside cylinders whereas piston valves had to go above or below, and piston valves were preferred by many designers for superheated engines because of lubrication considerations. With big cylinders, putting the valves above meant raising the boiler, possibly with attendant loading gauge problems. Faced with these limitations, piston valves below the cylinders were an understandable design option. Unfortunately, it meant that straight, wide steam passages were difficult to arrange for both admission and exhaust. Despite the proven advantages of long-lap, long-travel valves, J.E.Anderson was of the opinion that their wear and ensuing maintenance costs outweighed the advantages economically. The above is far from a detailed examination of the factors affecting the design of the '483s' but is offered to give some indication that common perceptions of design faults are often oversimplified. The men who schemed the engines were not simpletons who didn't understand how steam locomotives worked, which is the impression given by some commentators. Not only does hindsight clarify things wonderfully, it often results in misplaced arrogance in those who acquire it.

12. Of the engines selected to have their Schmidt rings replaced, the Compounds were probably the least affected by them. At least steam leakage past the high-pressure piston valves would end up in the low-pressure receiver and still be available to do some useful work in the

low-pressure cylinders, which had slide valves and, therefore, did not suffer the same problem. Leakage past the valves of simple expansion engines, however, merely escaped to atmosphere and contributed nothing to the engine's performance.

13. We have seen stated opinion that the low maintenance and repair costs of the engines would not have been as impressive had the cost per ton/mile of work done been taken into account. It is our understanding, however, that the basis of the 1926 calculations was just that.

14. There is a well-known coloured postcard of No. 483 in the Locomotive Publishing Co. collection, No. LPC/9, that is at variance with what we have written. From the information we have gathered, it appears that the artist who tinted it made a number of mistakes.

15. Although 'makers' plates' or 'works plates' are commonly used enthusiasts' terms, the Midland referred to them as 'name plates'. However, we feel that this is likely to cause confusion and so will continue to use the more familiar term of 'makers' plates'.

16. The reason for moving the running number from the tender to the locomotive cab sides was largely to enable tender exchanges to be carried out without altering the numbers. Derby practice had been to keep locomotives and tenders together when they went into the works for repair, which meant that there had to be a tender for each engine. Crewe, however, merely took the first suitable tender when a locomotive had completed its time in the works and attached it. Since tenders took less time to overhaul, there needn't be as many of them.

17. Changes to locomotive livery for reasons of economy were nothing new even when the Midland changed to black goods engines. Johnson's change from green for all locomotives in 1883 was the result of an attempt to find a less fugitive colour that would last better and extend the time between repaints.